People Like Us Can't

From bricklayer to nurse to doctor

in post-war Scotland

The Author—Graduation 1972

People Like Us Can't

From bricklayer to nurse
to doctor in post-war Scotland

Volume 1:
Memoirs of a Brickie
From Blantyre

James Graham

CreateSpace

People Like Us Can't

Copyright © James Graham 2015

The right of James Graham to be recognised as the author of this work is asserted by him in accordance with the Copyright, Designs and Patents Act 1988.

Disclaimer

This book is a work of non-fiction based on the life, experiences and recollections of the author. The names of various people and one or two places and events have been changed in the interests of confidentiality or to protect the privacy of others. Any similarities to real individuals with the names I've given them are entirely coincidental.

The following people are accorded their real names:

All relatives.
Miss Hardie, Miss Locke and Miss Whyte: matrons of Hairmyres Hospital, Victoria Infirmary and Philipshill Hospital respectively.
Miss Sclater, senior tutor at Hairmyres Hospital.
Miss Gunn, deputy matron at Philipshill Hospital.
Sisters Thomson and McLean at Hairmyres Hospital.
Sister McQueen at Philipshill Hospital.
Staff Nurse Ann McLean at Philipshill Hospital.
Bob Murray, Charge Nurse at Philipshill Hospital.
Mr Archie MacDougall, senior consultant orthopaedic surgeon at Victoria Infirmary and Philipshill Hospital.
Dr Olaf Kerr, consultant physician at the Western Infirmary.

Acknowledgements

My thanks are due to the following people and oganisations for assistance in the preparation of this work:

Richard Stenlake of Stenlake Publishing for permission to reproduce the image of Broompark Road, the place of my birth, from Old Blantyre. I have used this image on the cover and inside.

Keith Beattie manager of Ballymoney Museum, Co.Antrim for permission to use the image of The Reeling Room and Balnamore Mill.

Steve Younger minister of High Blantyre Baptist Church for supplying images and permission to use the image of the Wee Tin Kirk.

Alistair Tough and NHS Greater Glasgow and Clyde Archives, Mitchell Library, Glasgow for permission to use the sketch of Philipshill Hospital (H23/14/5) and the photograph of Miss Hardie, Matron of Hairmyres Hospital. (HD 28/12/18).

Barbara McLean and Glasgow City Archives, Mitchell Library, Glasgow for permission to use the image of Ward 1, Glasgow Eye Infirmary after the fire (ref. TD1431/51/49).

University of Glasgow Archivist for permission to use the Image of Bute Hall (ref. GB0248 PHU4/18).

The Cornfield Family for permission to use extracts from their late father's poems: *Colliers Every Wan* and *You Can't Take The Man Out of The Street*.

James Whelan for permission to use his poem *Quest of Life*.

Bill Sim of Blantyre's Ain website for permission to use two of his images.
http://www.blantyre.biz/Blantyre.html

Dea Parkin of Fiction Feedback (www.fictionfeedback.co.uk) for valuable advice, copy-editing and proofreading my work.

Dedication

To my beloved wife Mary, without whose support I would never have pursued my goal, and to my family, Eunice and Norman, without whose encouragement I would not have completed the book.

Contents

Chapter 1

Who Am I?
Where Did I Come From?

'People like us can't be doctors. We don't have the brains for that,' was my mother's response when I said I would like to be a doctor. My father's response was more judgemental.

'Don't try to get above your station in life, sir. Pride comes before a fall.'

Why? I was doing well at school and they received good reports from my teachers. Maybe my family's past, where we'd come from, explains in part.

Southern Scotland

Let me take you to a scenic part of Scotland, the Southern Uplands and in particular the Lowther Hills. The journey through these beautiful hills is by Mennock Pass to the west and Dalveen Pass to the east. However, running north-west to south-east for about six miles is another pass joining these two broader roads. It is Enterkin Pass, a narrow track with a steep drop to the

1

side in places. It is wide enough for a single horse and rider only. At the north-western end are the lead-mining villages of Wanlockhead and Leadhills, and a couple of miles beyond the south-eastern end is the farming village of Durisdeer. Enterkin Pass is now part of the Southern Upland Way.

Wanlockhead, the highest village in Scotland at 1,531 feet, is best known for lead mining but was once known as God's Treasure House because it was also a source of zinc, copper, silver and gold. Indeed it had the world's purest gold at 22.8 carats. This gold was used to make the crown for the coronation of Scottish kings.

In 1940s Wanlockhead, with no electricity, no television and use of the battery-operated radio severely restricted, our family would gather in a living room lit only by the fire in the evenings. Mum, Dad, Aunt Jean and Uncle Tom, and their elderly relatives, would reminisce on times gone by. Two themes and one place recurred frequently, often in vivid detail. The themes were the Covenanters and the resurrectionists and the place was Enterkin Pass. It is at times beautiful, especially in sunshine; and at times ghostly and frightening, especially at dawn or dusk when the frequent mists come down. These mists are not simply a light haze but a dense fog, almost like the pea-soupers of the industrial cities but without the pollution. F. H. Groome, in *Ordinance Gazetteer of Scotland (1882–4)* says,

> *It is followed along all its course by the old Leadhills bridle-path from Clydesdale into*

Nithsdale . . . that famous Enterkin Pass. A few steps and you are on its edge, looking down giddy and amazed into its sudden and immense depth. . . . We have seen many of our glens and mountain gorges . . . all kinds of beauty and sublimity but we know nothing more noticeable, more like any other place, than this short, deep, narrow and sudden glen. There is only room for its own stream at the bottom, and the side rises in one smooth and all but perpendicular ascent to the height, on the left, of 1895 feet in Thirstane Hill, and, on the right, of 1875 feet in the exquisitely moulded Stey Gail, or Steep Gable, so steep that it is no easy matter keeping your feet, and if you slip you might just as well go over a bona fide mural precipice.[1]

The Covenanters

Following the Union of crowns in 1603, the Stuart kings tried to impose the Anglican system of church government, where the king was also the head of the Church, on Presbyterian Scotland. Presbyterians resolved to resist

---

[1] GB Historical GIS / University of Portsmouth, Durisdeer ScoP through time / Census tables with data for the Scottish Parish. *A Vision of Britain through Time.*
URL: http://www.visionofbritain.org.uk/unit/10051083 .

this and a National Covenant was signed pledging allegiance to King Charles I, but demanding that he honour his father's promise to uphold the Presbyterian Church, a free Scottish Parliament and Scottish laws. This was tantamount to a declaration of rebellion and Charles's armies attacked Scotland. In the latter part of the ensuing persecution, known as *the killing times,* the Covenanters were forced into remote hills and glens especially in southern Scotland to conduct their services, known as conventicles, in the open air.

The gatherings were small at the beginning but grew in size, often with more than a thousand attending. The ministers and many of the congregations had to live as outlaws with soldiers hunting them down. Those caught were taken to Edinburgh for trial. Some were sent to the colonies or forced to work as galley slaves on ships and many were executed on the Maiden, an early form of guillotine.

Great covenanting preachers such as Alexander Peden featured in the stories we heard in Wanlockhead. He was known as Prophet Peden because he seemed to have an uncanny ability to know when the king's soldiers were about to appear and thus enable his congregation to escape before they arrived. On one occasion he hid in the heather and his head was grazed by the hoof of one of the soldier's horses but he remained undiscovered. James Renwick was another Covenanter from Dumfries-shire who was captured and taken to Edinburgh where he was executed in 1688. Peden, Renwick and others preached in the Lowther Hills and frequently in and around Mennock Pass, Dalveen Pass and Enterkin Pass.

In one story, sixteen Covenanters including their minister had been caught and were being taken through a very misty Enterkin Pass by twenty-eight soldiers to Edinburgh for trial and probable execution when another group of Covenanters tried to rescue them. They waited till the soldiers and their prisoners were on a high, narrow part of the pass with a steep drop to the side. Suddenly from the hillside, the waiting rescuers called out to the soldiers below them.

'Give us our minister,' they shouted. The officer in charge refused and the leader of the rescuers shot him in the head, so he fell dead into the abyss below. The rest of the soldiers, afraid of suffering a similar fate, fled, letting the prisoners go free, although a few were recaptured later.

Because the Covenanters were armed for their protection fights occurred between them and the soldiers. Often soldiers or Covenanters were killed in these skirmishes and because many of the bodies were never recovered the old folks believed their ghosts still wandered the hills and glens and could be seen and heard in the mist.

The Resurrectionists

In the eighteenth and nineteenth centuries with better education of doctors in training there was a great need for cadavers for the teaching of anatomy, and for surgeons to practise their art. Initially the bodies of executed criminals were used but supply proved inadequate so there grew up a trade in the sale of corpses. These entrepreneurs were the resurrectionists who watched the graveyards for burials taking place. Then they would return in the darkness at night and dig up the body to sell to prominent doctors.

My mother had a great fear of being buried alive and often said to us, 'Now you make sure I'm properly dead before you let them screw down the coffin lid. I don't want to wake up in a coffin.' She told us the story of a man during the time of the resurrectionists.

He had been ill for some time and fell into a coma, so the relatives called the doctor who examined him and said, 'I'm afraid he's dead.' The undertaker came and prepared him for burial by binding his feet and ankles together, tying his hands and wrists firmly to the side of his body as well as securing his mouth in a closed position with a bandage tied round his chin and head. They put him in the coffin and the funeral was arranged.

During the funeral service the poor man awoke from his coma to hear the sound of singing, and then the minister's muffled voice, but the man was unable to move or call out. He felt himself being carried and placed on a cart that was drawn by a horse over a rough track.

There was further talk and he thought he could hear among the muffled sounds the words, 'Ashes . . . dust . . . resurrection.' He could hear the sound of weeping and his worst fears were confirmed. He was at his own funeral service. Next he felt himself being lowered and there was a thud as soil was thrown on the coffin. There was quiet for a while and then more thuds of soil landing as the gravediggers filled in the grave.

He was panicking as he lay in silence knowing full well he would soon run out of oxygen and die for real this time, but after what seemed like eternity there was the sound of digging, and then the coffin lid was broken open and fresh air came in. Hands grasped him by the head and pulled him roughly upwards. He was thrown on the ground and then lifted on to a cart and trundled away to be handed over to the anatomist. As the doctor removed the ties that bound the 'corpse' ready to cut him open, the man, feeble and barely alive, let out a moan so that even the seasoned anatomist recoiled in horror.

The *specimen* was too weak to sit up but whispered a 'thank you' to the anatomist. Then almost immediately, he saw the implements for cutting him open and a feeling of despair engulfed him once again. Being aware that murder was a common means of obtaining bodies, he begged, 'Please don't kill me.' The morals of the anatomist are doubtful but there were witnesses, so he helped the man from the slab and gave him a drink of water. Trembling from weakness he realised he had indeed been saved and a great sense of relief engulfed him. The grieving relatives were contacted and could scarcely believe what they were being told. With trepidation his wife and son arrived at the anatomy department, but there was no doubt. Their husband and father was indeed alive and they took him home with great rejoicing.

Burke and Hare are the two most notorious early nineteenth century providers of corpses. They did not dig up graves but devised a means of murdering people without leaving a mark. Burke was the murderer and his method was to ply his victims with alcohol, and suffocate them when they were too drunk to resist. This came to be known as 'burking'. Hare then sold the bodies to Dr Robert Knox, an Edinburgh anatomist.

Burke and Hare were caught in 1828 and their last victim was found in the possession of Dr Knox whose reputation was ruined as a result, forcing him to leave Edinburgh. At the time of Burke and Hare's apprehension a street song became popular with children.

Burke's the butcher, Hare's the thief,
Knox the boy who buys the beef.

The methods of Burke and Hare were copied by other criminals throughout the country. Resurrected bodies and the victims of the murders from what is now Dumfries and Galloway were taken to Glasgow or Edinburgh and a favourite route was through Enterkin Pass.

Suicides

People who committed suicide in those days could not have a Christian burial so anyone from Wanlockhead or Leadhills who died as a result of suicide was taken up Lowther Hill to the summit in an old cart and dumped on the slope away from the villages. The cart was left there with the body but to anyone passing a few days later there was no sign either of the body or the cart. The rational explanation as accepted by Mum and Aunt Jean was that a resurrectionist came at night and brought the body back down to sell, but the more common explanation as accepted by our older relatives was that Old Meg, a witch in league with the devil, took them away and the ghost could be seen wandering the hills and glens in the mist or darkness. As though Enterkin Pass wasn't formidable enough, anyone going to Wanlockhead through the Pass had to climb the dumping grounds of Lowther Hill before descending to the village.

Maternal Family History

Unmarried Mother

My maternal great-grandmother, Janet Wright, was born on 27 August 1848. She was the daughter of a road worker, David Wright, from Durisdeer Mill, just south of Dalveen Pass on what is now the A702. Two years later my great-great-grandfather David became an agricultural labourer and moved the family to the village of Durisdeer about one mile further into the Durisdeer Hills. Aged twelve, after leaving school, Janet went to work as a dairy maid on a farm near the village.

She would almost certainly have been resident and taught by the farmer's wife the carefully guarded secrets of caring for the milk and cream as well as making butter and cheese. As a dairymaid, most of her work was in the dairy and mostly with other dairymaids. The women worked indoors and the men outdoors but the dairymaids and the dairymen did work together on the milking.

Shortly after her nineteenth birthday she had a nasty shock when she found herself pregnant, and pregnant by someone who wasn't prepared to accept responsibility. It's not known if she was exploited by a married landowner or perhaps one of his sons who wouldn't marry someone so far below his station in life. Equally it may have been a romp in the hay with a co-worker which went too far and the lad was unwilling to take on his responsibility. Either way she gave birth to my grandmother, Isabella Wright, on 27 May 1869. In place of a father's name on the birth certificate is the word 'illegitimate'. Despite the great shame associated with illegitimate births at that time, Janet's parents David and Isabella Wright displayed love and care for their daughter and granddaughter. Janet was allowed to stay at home in Tunnel Cottage, Durisdeer and have her baby there. Isabella was happy for her new granddaughter to take her name.

Meanwhile the wife of Janet's brother James died, leaving him with three children. He worked as a labourer and lived in the village of Morton a few miles away so Janet, with new baby Isabella, went to live with him as housekeeper. This was a help to Janet and James for a time but as nature took its course, James fell in love again and remarried, making Janet and her baby unwelcome. She had to find work and a place to live, but who would employ an unmarried girl with an infant? A solution was found when she gained employment as a domestic servant in Wanlockhead on the other side of the Lowther Hills. Her parents took their granddaughter Isabella, now two years of age, to live with them in Durisdeer.

To get to her place of employment and to return to her parents' home to see them and little Isabella on her one day off a month, Janet had to walk, very early in the morning and very late at night, through the frightening Enterkin Pass, of which Daniel Defoe said in *A Tour Through the Whole Island of Britain*:

> *. . . the wildest and most hideous aspect in all the south of Scotland; as particularly that of Enterkin, the frightfullest pass, and most dangerous that I met with, between that and Penmenmuir in North Wales.*[2]

Janet told how, on that first morning, she set off very early before daylight for the eight-mile walk from Durisdeer to Wanlockhead. Dawn was breaking as she entered the pass and there was heavy mist as she approached the point where it was thought the Covenanters had ambushed the soldiers and shot the officer in

---

[2] GB Historical GIS / University of Portsmouth, Durisdeer ScoP through time / Census tables with data for the Scottish Parish. *A Vision of Britain through Time*.
URL: http://www.visionofbritain.org.uk/unit/10051083

charge. She had heard tales of his ghost appearing in search of his prisoners. As she passed the point there were strange shapes appearing out of the mist and her heart was pounding as she climbed the hill. She tried to run but her legs could barely move as though she was in a bad dream. The shapes followed her, accompanied by a strange low moaning sound, and she became convinced these were the ghosts of the officer and his men, but as she climbed higher and was almost at the point of exhaustion the mist cleared and the 'ghosts' disappeared. Calmer now, she continued towards her destination.

On another occasion when she was making her way from Wanlockhead back to Durisdeer she climbed Lowther Hill in the darkness just before dawn. There had been a suicide and the poor woman taken up the hill to be dumped the day before. Janet was aware of the tales about Old Meg, the witch who roamed the hills and collected the bodies of suicides for the devil. She never knew whether to believe them or not but they seemed very real to her when she was alone on the hills in the mist and darkness.

As she reached the summit and was about to descend towards Enterkin Pass she heard heavy breathing and grunting and could just make out shapes in the mist ahead. Was this Old Meg with the devil taking the body away, or the ghost of the suicide victim? She tried to run but this could be dangerous in the mist and darkness and after a few yards she tripped and fell. As she tried to get up a hand appeared out of the mist and pulled her to her feet.

Terrified she said, 'Who are you? Please don't harm me.'

'You don't need to know who I am,' a man replied, 'but don't worry, I'm not interested in the living, only the dead.' By this time there was just enough daylight for her to make out the shape of a scruffy-looking man and an old cart with what looked like a body on it. Poor Janet was terrified and she still had to walk all the way through Enterkin Pass, but as the daylight increased, the mist lifted and the sun shone she was able to realise that the tales of Old Meg were just tales. Instead, she had encountered a resurrectionist taking the body away to sell it.

There were many occasions when Janet was afraid walking alone through Enterkin Pass but her love for little Isabella and her parents motivated her to keep going. The walk could be pleasant on clear sunny days and there was one such occasion when she was walking back to Wanlockhead on a summer evening. It was unusual for her to meet another person on the long lonely walk but on this occasion as two paths met, she became aware of two men joining and walking behind her. She became anxious and quickened her pace as she walked towards Enterkin Pass and for a time they appeared to drop back, but then their pace quickened and they kept at the same distance behind her.

Although it was light at this point she still had two hours of walking through that lonely, scary pass and it would be dark before she left it. Having grown up with the stories of Burke and Hare, the thought occurred to her that she was about to be murdered and her body sold for anatomy lectures in Glasgow or Edinburgh. Although Burke and Hare were both dead by then she was convinced that the murders were still happening.

She ran a bit and increased the distance between herself and the men a little, but soon tired and had to walk again. After a time, dusk and the mist, which had caused so much fear at other times, now gave her some cover, and she kept going, waiting for her opportunity. She had heard tales of Prophet Peden's hiding places when being pursued by the king's soldiers and knew of one such place ahead. When she reached a steep-sided valley she ran in there and hid in a gulley, barely daring to breathe as she heard the two men walk past. Once certain they were well on their way she started on her journey again but this time walking very slowly to keep a good distance behind them. On reflection years later she was sure the men were completely innocent and she had let her imagination run riot, but who could blame her?

Marriage

During her time as a servant in Wanlockhead Janet met a young lead miner, James McCall. They fell in love and were married in December 1873 in Tunnel Cottage, Durisdeer. This was the cottage where she had given birth to Isabella four and a half years earlier. Isabella's mum and new stepfather took her to live with them in Wanlockhead so Janet's regular early morning and late night walks through Enterkin Pass came to an end.

James and Janet went on to have seven more children but only four survived childhood. Janet died at the age of sixty-one in Glasgow Royal Infirmary. The cause of death was recorded as gallstones.

High Blantyre

Isabella, my grandmother, had a happy childhood in Wanlockhead with several half brothers and sisters. When she left school aged twelve she was employed as a domestic servant in the village. Meanwhile John Watson, the son of a lead miner, Thomas Watson, was starting work as a labourer in one of the lead mines. They met and fell in love but unfortunately the mine in which John was working closed and he had to move away to find work.

His cousin was living in Blantyre, Lanarkshire and John went there to lodge with the cousin while he found work. He worked as a general labourer at first but later found work as a coal miner in High Blantyre. This was shortly after a terrible mining disaster which killed over two hundred men and boys. He went back to Wanlockhead to marry my grandmother in March 1895, after which they set up home in High Blantyre. They had six children, two of whom died in infancy.

My Mother

My mother was the fourth and youngest of the surviving children. She was born on 23 June 1904 and named

Margaret Fraser McCall Watson. I know where the Margaret, McCall and Watson come from but there is no record of a Fraser in either my grandfather's or grandmother's ancestry.

My grandparents followed the usual protocols for naming children at that time. With daughters that meant the first girl named after the maternal grandmother and the second daughter after the paternal grandmother. Mum as the third daughter was given her stepgrandfather's name, McCall, as a second middle name, but Fraser? In some cases in the nineteenth century an illegitimate child would be given the biological father's surname as a middle name but not in Isabella's case. Had Janet at some point told Isabella who her biological father was and she decided to pass it on?

When Mum left school she applied for work as a domestic servant. One day as she was helping her mother with the cleaning and was down on her knees scrubbing out the cupboard under the sink with the contents scattered around her on the floor, her prospective employer appeared at the door unannounced to interview her. My mother and grandmother were so embarrassed and apologised profusely for the mess, thinking, there goes any chance of this job. However the lady was very impressed at this level of thoroughness and my mother got the job.

My grandfather, Grandpa Watson, had little religious inclination but my grandmother was a member of High Blantyre Baptist Church. She took her children there too, and they continued as members of the Baptist Church until they were married.

Ireland

I had always been vaguely aware of an Irish connection in my paternal ancestry but was never given any details. On researching my ancestry I went back to my paternal great-great-grandparents who were Irish, and noted that my great-great-grandfather was a Graham married to an Armstrong. My great-grandfather married an Atkinson. However, none of these is a native Irish name, so how did they get to Ireland? To understand this we need to look at British and Irish history and I've provided a brief outline on my website: www.ascottishdoctor.com/who-am-i

Examination of my ancestry and DNA analysis suggests that I am descended from the Border Reivers through the Grahams and the Armstrongs. The Border Reivers were marauding bands who operated in the lawless no-man's-land between England and Scotland between the fourteenth and seventeenth centuries with the Grahams operating mainly on the English side of the present border and the Armstrongs on the Scottish. They were probably deported to Ireland by James VI of Scotland (James I of England and Ireland) in the seventeenth century.

Paternal Family History

Famine in Ireland

My paternal great-great-grandparents John and Mary (nee Armstrong) Graham were tenant farmers in Bally-money, Co. Antrim, Ireland. In the Great Irish Famine of 1840–1851, it is said that a million people died of starvation and disease and about two million emigrated. The Graham family, as with so many tenant farmers, were

Image 1-1: Balnamore Mill now derelict.
Courtesy of Ballymoney Museum, Co. Antrim.

starving and unable to pay their rent. Mary was pregnant in 1845 when they were forced off their land and found themselves homeless.

This poor yet proud couple who had worked the land all their lives were forced into the city, Belfast, to find inadequate, cramped, squalid accommodation for their family. They moved to the Shankill area but other people in a similar situation were pouring in from the rural areas and typhus was rife. By 1847 it was claiming fifty lives a day in Shankill alone.

It was there that my great-grandfather, also John Graham, was born. His father was still unemployed and the family in desperate straits until he eventually found

Image 1-2: Reeling Room, Balnamore Mill.
Courtesy of Ballymoney Museum, Co. Antrim.

work as a weaver in Balnamore Mill, Co. Antrim which was one of the largest spinning mills outside Belfast. The wages he earned were just about enough to enable them to rent a small cottage nearer the mill in Ballymoney and away from the squalor, disease and death in the city.

My other Irish great-great-grandparents, John and Sarah Atkinson, were also tenant farmers. They farmed in Tamlaght, Finlagan, Co. Derry and they too found themselves unable to pay the rent and were evicted. Like many Irish tenant farmers at this time they had nowhere to go so they squatted in their former home living on scraps of food they found around the farm.

My great-grandmother, also Sarah, was born there in 1847. The landlord eventually forced them out but fortunately they avoided the indignity of squalid accommodation in the city and were able to rent a small cottage in Balnamore, close to the mill after John Atkinson too found employment there as a weaver. Although conditions in the mill were harsh and dangerous, in later years many recalled their time there with some affection because the 'craic' was good and there was a strong sense of community.

As soon as their children were old enough, aged twelve, they went to work in the mill. It was there that John Graham (my great-grandfather) met Sarah Atkinson (my great-grandmother) as children working in that dusty and dangerous environment. As they grew into their teens their relationship blossomed and they were married in October 1866 in the Church of Ireland at Ballymoney.

Over the Sea to Scotland

Towards the end of 1867 my great-grandfather John found himself out of work with little or no prospect of finding another job and Sarah was pregnant with their first child. The baby, William (Dad's Uncle Willie), was born in January 1868 and following his Church of

Ireland baptism in February the family soon set sail for Scotland where John found work as a boatyard labourer in Greenock on the Firth of Clyde.

Their second child Elizabeth (Lizzie) was born in March 1869 and the family were now struggling to make ends meet on John's labourer's wages. Greenock had a number of sugar refineries where he was able to get work as a labourer and it was while he was working there that my grandfather James Graham was born in November 1872.

Work in sugar refineries was hot, exhausting and dangerous with frequent serious injuries and fatal accidents. There were no Safety at Work Regulations and accidents were always blamed on the workers; never the owners. Accidents and fatalities comprised incidents such as: 'falling into boiling water when cleaning sugar vats'; 'scalded with boiling sugar'; 'roof fell in'; 'rope ladder on which they were working gave way causing a fall from great height'; 'a fall into boiling sugar' and 'boilers exploding causing serious injury or death.' Very often the cause of death was not specified but simply recorded as 'accident in sugar factory'. Suicides were common.

Back to Ireland

After several years of this the family returned to Ireland where my great-grandfather found employment as a farm labourer back in Ballymoney. Their decision to leave Scotland was partly due to the difficult and dangerous nature of the work in the sugar refinery and partly due to the resentment shown by native Scots, because Irish labours were willing to work for much lower wages and so took their jobs, but mainly because the Irish economy was starting to improve.

Return to Scotland

The two sons, William, Dad's Uncle Willie and James, my grandfather, returned to Scotland in their late teens in search of work. Great Uncle Willie settled in Langholm in the Scottish Borders where he worked as a woodman, and Grandfather came to High Blantyre and found work in the mines. He was a colliery stoker at first and later progressed to winding engineman.

Like my other grandfather, John Watson, he arrived at the High Blantyre coal mines shortly after the 1877 disaster. Although born in Scotland, he was born of Irish parents and had grown up in Ireland, acquiring an Irish accent, so he met the same hostility from the native Scots as his father had before him in Greenock. The religious tensions of Ireland had a significant impact too. James Cornfield, himself a Blantyre miner and descended from relatives of victims, referred to these difficulties in his poem, in the Blantyre dialect, about the mining disaster, as shown in the following extract:

**Colliers Every Wan
(In memory of the Blantyre Disaster,
22nd October 1877)**

They came fae Erin this family o' mine,
Tae Scotia's fair land tae work underground.
Wi' promise o' plenty ringin' in thur ears,
They fun' only poverty, blood, sweat an' tears.

Nothing hid changed at the end o' the day,
Same bosses, same serfdom, same low pay.
The local Scotchmen didnae like them at aw',
Fur they took aw' thur joabs an' thur hooses in the
Raw.

Different religions didnae help them as well,
In fact it wis jist like livin' in Hell.
Trouble in Pit, mair when they came hame,
Thur wir times when they wished they'd never
came.

But aw' this wid change wi' the passage o' time,
When fate took a hand doon there in that mine.
A build up o' gas, a wee naked flame,
An' maist o' these colliers wid never go hame.

The horn oan the Pithead blew long an' forlorn,
Tae signal bad news that fateful morn.
Folk came runnin' fae aw' o'er the toon,
Every wan tae a man, volunteered tae go doon.

23

Nae thought o' danger, nor religion too,
They aw' worked thegither wi' a common view.
The fellowship o' man was born that day,
In Blantir toon, how I wish it wid stay.

Two hundred and sixteen colliers lay dead,
Killed in pursuit o' thur daily bread.
Men, boys an' uncles, brithers an aw',
Wid never return tae thur hoose in the Raw.[3]

James Cornfield 2002

Romance and Marriage

Despite the difficulties of travel at that time there was considerable movement between different mining communities, and my grandmother Janet Anderson came with her parents to Blantyre from the mining village of Shotts in Lanarkshire. She married my grandfather in April 1898 and their firstborn, my father John, was born on 6 April 1899.

My Father

After leaving school aged fourteen my father followed him into the mines. Sadly in 1921 my grandfather died, aged only forty-eight, from bronchiectasis (lung abscess), no doubt from the effects of inhaled coal dust. By

---

[3] *Colliers Every Wan*, James Cornfield 2002, Changing Places published by Changing Places Blantyre.

this time my father had already had one episode of life-threatening pneumonia with pleurisy and was developing a chronic cough, so he decided to get out of coal mining. He found work as a bricklayers' labourer building *homes fit for heroes* after the First World War.

Although my grandparents James and Janet were members of the Free Church of Scotland my father rejected religion and was an atheist with leanings towards communism. However around the age of twenty-seven he began to be troubled by the thought that he might be wrong. One day when he was walking through a field he picked up a wild flower and marvelled at the exquisite design. He thought, a design must have a designer, and decided to be a Christian.

I have never heard him discuss the background to this but I do know he had read widely before his conversion. He had a small bookcase with a variety of books including *The Voyage of the Beagle* and *The Origin of Species* by Charles Darwin. Others I recall were *Les Miserables* by Victor Hugo and works by Voltaire. I wonder if this idea of design in nature was influenced by the famous book by William Paley (1743–1805), *Natural Theology,* in which he used the analogy of finding a watch among stones. The stones were there naturally, he thought, but concluded that for there to be a watch with its intricate design there must be a watchmaker. So design in nature must have a designer. The well-known evangelist for atheism, Prof Richard Dawkins, argues against this in his book *The Blind Watchmaker.* His arguments are in turn refuted by many prominent

Christian writers including Prof Alastair McGrath, Prof Keith Ward and John Cornwell.

After converting to Christianity my father went round the local churches in search of a spiritual home and while visiting High Blantyre Baptist Church he met a pretty little lass, Maggie Watson. They took a liking to each other and the friendship blossomed into romance. Although he didn't settle in the Baptist Church, their romance continued.

After trying a few more churches he visited the Christian Brethren who had their gospel hall in High Blantyre. While deciding if this was the church for him he was sitting one Sunday looking at a Bible text displayed at the front. It was the words of Jesus when hanging from the cross and read, 'It is finished, John 19:30.' However part of it was obscured from his view by the lectern and what he saw was, 'It is finished, John.' He took this as a sign that the Brethren Church was the place for him and settled there. The Brethren and the Baptists were theologically similar, the main difference being that Baptists had ordained ministers and Brethren had lay preachers, but they were on good terms and co-operated in joint services.

Chapter 2
Home and Family

Parents' Marriage

John and Maggie's relationship flourished and they were married by Pastor Wilson, the founder of High Blantyre Baptist Church, in the Manse on 22 September 1933.

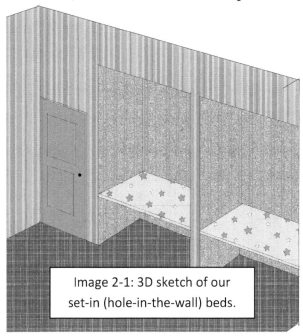

Image 2-1: 3D sketch of our set-in (hole-in-the-wall) beds.

They found a single-end tenement flat to rent at 66 Broompark Road, High Blantyre. John continued to work as a bricklayers' labourer in the building boom between the two World Wars, building what were termed *homes fit for heroes*. Maggie continued to work as a domestic servant for a year but stopped working during her first pregnancy.

Their first child, my sister Isabel, was born on 16 February 1935 and I followed three years later on 1 March 1938. Their third and final child, my brother John, was born four years after me on 14 March 1942. We were all born at home in a *set-in* or *hole-in-the-wall* bed in the single end in Broompark Road. My mother often spoke of Mrs Welsh, the midwife who came to deliver us.

Delivering babies in hole-in-the-wall beds was no mean feat for the mother or the midwife but it was common practice in tenements all over the country. This was a time when childbirth was very hazardous and there was a saying among older women: 'It's a bed you go into but you don't know if you'll come out alive.' Around four mothers and thirty babies died for every thousand births.

The Tenement

I was born eighteen months before the outbreak of the Second World War and named James after my paternal grandfather. My earliest memories are of the war years with a coal fire burning in the range. The heavy wooden shutters were closed in case the warden came by and saw any light from the window. Our tenement had no gas or electricity so the room was rather dimly lit by a paraffin lamp. Cooking was done on the range or on a paraffin

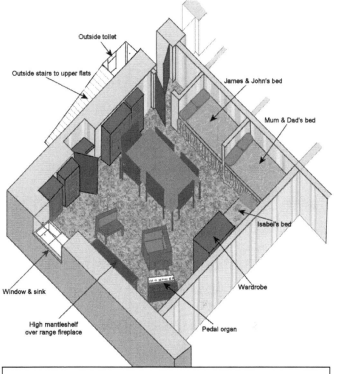

Image 2-2: 3D sketch of our single-end tenement flat.

stove, and I look back in admiration at what my mother achieved with the most basic of facilities. An electricity supply was eventually put in but not till I was about eleven years of age.

The one room, which must have been about 18 feet square, had two hole-in-the-wall beds which were about

3 feet above the floor with a curtain covering the storage space underneath. There was a single bed adjacent to them, a sideboard, a wardrobe, a chest of drawers, a pedal organ and an extending table in the centre of the room, as well as a cupboard built into the wall. My parents shared one hole-in-the-wall bed and John and I shared the other. Isabel had the separate single bed.

Many homes had pedal organs then, especially religious homes. They were about the size of a small upright piano and the bellows were driven by two foot pedals.

There was a sink at the one window with cold running water but no hot. The floor was covered by linoleum, or 'wax cloth' as my mother called it, and there was a small rug at the fireside. The one armchair beside the fire was Father's when he was in and Mum used to sit in it to do her darning or sewing after he went to bed. Just occasionally she managed to have a little time to herself reading one of her two magazines, the *Christian Herald* and *The Weekly News*. The light for this came from the Aladdin paraffin lamp on the high mantelshelf. She was so tired by this time that she usually fell asleep when trying to read her magazines.

We had an outside toilet which we shared with another family but we were fortunate because it was just outside the door. The other family had to walk all the way round the building summer and winter. There was the standard high cistern with a long chain and the *wally*, or porcelain toilet pan with a strip of wood fixed on either side to sit on. A nail had been hammered into the wall and attached to this was string with four-to-six-inch squares of newspaper. I had never heard of toilet roll but when fruit from overseas came into the shops after the war, a more luxurious substitute toilet paper also became available in limited quantities. The fruit, especially oranges and apples, was individually wrapped in a lightly waxed soft tissue paper and this was fought over for the toilet. In our family the issue of who could use it was quickly resolved. Dad had to have it for his piles.

A candle was the light source in the toilet on dark nights. In winter the pipes, being outside, were always at risk of freezing, not to mention our bottoms. Mum put a small paraffin heater in when the temperature fell below freezing point. It wasn't enough to make us feel warm but avoided the dreaded loss of water supply and the inevitable burst pipes when the thaw came.

Although we lived in tenements they were quite well spaced out. To the front of the building was the road, Broompark Road, and to the back there was an area of hard soil, referred to as the back court, between the building and the coal cellars and wash house. Behind them was a field belonging to Rockhead's farm. To one side overlooked by our window was another of the farmer's fields and to the other side was the communal drying green and beyond a branch railway line. The farm was on the further side of this and we sometimes crossed the rails to get there.

Our coal was delivered by the local coalman once a week and whatever we could afford had to last till the following week. We had a few coal miners in the building and they had their free coal delivered by the ton. They never appeared to have any shortage and many were quite generous, so it wasn't uncommon for a miner's neighbour, usually where the husband was ill, to appear with an old pram and be given some of their coal.

Laundry was done in the shared outside wash house with each family allocated one half-day per week either morning or afternoon. We had a Wednesday morning and my mother would get up at 4 am, when my father was leaving for work, and had the washing done by 8 am.

At some point during my childhood my father left the building industry and became a bread delivery man. He had a horse-drawn van and a team of two Clydesdale horses with which he delivered his bread round the shops in the Gorbals district of Glasgow. In later years he was given an electric van and eventually graduated to petrol.

Quite frequently on dark winter Wednesday mornings Mum would ask me to come with her for company and help with some of the fetching and carrying. There was a coal-fired boiler in one corner of the wash house and two washing tubs, one with a scrubbing board for washing and one for rinsing, which had a wringer or mangle. The clothes were dried on the communal back green when the weather was dry and on the pulley over the table in the middle of the room when it was wet.

The mother of the family whose use of the wash house followed ours usually came to Mum and asked her to leave the hot water in the boiler and the tubs for her use. She obviously thought we were clean enough for her to use our second-hand water, and it saved on the coal.

Plots

During the war and in the post-war years, the government encouraged people to cultivate any available ground to grow food for themselves. There was an area around the perimeter of the green sectioned off to give each family a plot of ground for this purpose. There was one longer section along one edge where an upstairs neighbour, Mr Brown kept hens. He often got very cross if we were too noisy or kicked a ball against the wire fence. On one occasion when I was watching another neighbour, Mr Murphy, digging his plot, he was unaware of my presence and threw a slate over his shoulder hitting me on the head. I needed stitches and still have the scar.

An air-raid shelter was situated at the far end of the green adjacent to the railway line and we went there when there were air-raid warnings, sometimes in the middle of the night.

Collectors

Friday was payday for most working people and there was usually a procession of collectors doing their rounds on a Friday evening in an attempt to get their money before it was spent. First in line was the rent man, generally referred to as the factor. Another regular was the Society man who collected the insurance money. I assume this was insurance for the household contents and life insurance to cover funeral costs. His name was Andrew Reid and he had something in common with my parents since he was a member of High Blantyre Baptist Church. Debt collectors always made Friday their main collection day too.

Surrounding Homes

Looking back at the variety of houses in our small area, the perceived hierarchy was interesting. We lived in a single end in a tenement and we considered that to be

View as it is today from where our tenement was:
Homes fit for heroes in front
Gates to villa on left

Image 2-3: View across Broompark Road to Springfield Cr.

the norm. Across the road was a detached villa with upstairs attic bedrooms and it had a fairly long drive. We thought it was very posh but as children we later made friends with the two sons of the Quinn family who lodged in the attic. They were just like us but renting rooms in a private house, and any time we went to the house to play with them Mrs Quinn was anxious in case we made too much noise and upset the landlord who lived on the ground floor.

One day during the war years there was a loud grating sound, and I ran out to the road to see men working on the iron railings of the villa. They were using a flame to cut through the railings and then grinding the ends to smooth them off.

I ran back into the house and said to Mum, 'There are men over there stealing Bob Bell's railings.'

She replied, 'No, don't worry, the men aren't stealing, they're taking all the railings away because the government needs all the metal they can get to make things like guns, bullets and ships for the war.'

Adjacent to this villa was Springfield Crescent with neat semi-detached bungalows on either side, each with its own gate, pathway and front and back garden. There were a few on Broompark Road too, seen on the right in the foreground of Image 2-4. We thought the people who lived in them must be posh too and they certainly acted in a superior manner.

We walked that way going to and from our primary school and we were aware of eyes peering behind curtains waiting to pounce on us for any misdemeanours such as being pushed against the hedge by friends. Any time we played on the pavement or road nearby we were always chased away with comments such as, 'You boys get back to your tenements and stop making a noise in our quarter.' However there must have been times when their annoyance was justified, especially when we played KDRF, *knock doors run fast*. In fact they were simply people who had been fortunate enough to get a council

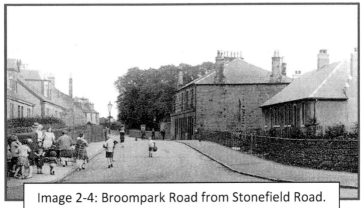

Image 2-4: Broompark Road from Stonefield Road.
Our tenement is on the left in the background.
From *Old Blantyre* courtesy of Stenlake Publishing.

house in what had been part of the government's *homes fit for heroes* building programme after the First World War, but which slowed to a stop as the economy weakened in the 1920s. There were also a few privately owned stone villas adjacent to the tenements, seen on the left in the foreground of Image 2-4.

Going down Stonefield Road to Low Blantyre we passed Dixon's Rows. We called them *the Raws*. These were rows of terraced houses for miners, all closely packed together. Each had two rooms, one a bedroom and the other serving as living room, kitchen and bedroom. We were sorry for the people who lived there and thought they were poor compared with us. Ironically, I later learned that they considered their homes to be the norm and were sorry for the poor people like us who lived in the tenements.

Just on the other side of the railway line was Rockhead's Farm, and on the opposite side of Broompark Road from the farm was a large, very grand, detached villa which looked like a castle to us, situated in spacious grounds including a tennis court. This was the home of local GPs; Dr Jope the husband and Dr Jope the wife. They had a large chestnut tree close to the perimeter wall and we always went there to get chestnuts to play *chessies* in the autumn. When we couldn't find good ones outside the wall we would sneak inside through the gate. We usually managed to avoid being seen but occasionally the gardener caught us and dragged us by the scruffs of our necks back outside the gate.

The doctors used part of the house as a branch surgery, their primary surgery being at Main Street, High Blantyre. For some time they had a live-in servant who had a son the same age as me and my mother befriended her. She came to visit Mum when she had some time off. John and I occasionally went to the big house to play with her son but we were only allowed to play in their own very cramped quarters. We did go outside to play in the spacious grounds once but were chased by Mrs Jope and told to get back to the servants' quarters.

Grandfather lived in a similar tenement to ours about 200 yards away, (the one nearest on the right after the new houses in Image 2-4), and my mother went to check on him a few times a day. With no street lighting allowed during the war years she often asked me to go with her for company on dark evenings. The sky was sometimes bright and starlit and I remember gazing up in wonder at the dazzling display of twinkling little lights, and we would sing the only two verses we knew of the song by Ann and Jane Taylor:

Twinkle, twinkle, little star,
How I wonder what you are.
Up above the world so high,
Like a diamond in the sky.

In the dark blue sky you keep,
And often through my curtains peep,
For you never shut your eye,
'Till the sun is in the sky.

We learned a poem by Walter De La Mare about the moon and had to paint a picture of the scene at Primary School. I often recited it on a clear moonlit night as we walked to Grandfather's.

Silver
Slowly, silently, now the moon
Walks the night in her silver shoon;
This way, and that, she peers, and sees
Silver fruit upon silver trees;
One by one the casements catch

Her beams beneath the silvery thatch;
Couched in his kennel, like a log,
With paws of silver sleeps the dog;
From their shadowy cote the white breasts peep
Of doves in a silver-feathered sleep
A harvest mouse goes scampering by,
With silver claws and a silver eye;
And moveless fish in the water gleam,
By silver reeds in a silver stream.

On a cloudy night it could be very dark indeed and quite scary walking past the unlit gas lamps. A small torch was allowed so long as it was always pointed downwards. On nights with a full moon the adults were usually anxious because the German bomber crews could see and follow the River Clyde. The targets were the power stations and steelworks near the Clyde, and of course the shipyards on the river.

Clydebank on the other side of Glasgow was bombed mercilessly during the Blitz. We were aware of the drone of the heavy bomber engines as they approached, followed by the explosions, and then the sky lighting up with ensuing fires. My mother-in-law to be was deaf due to the blast from a bomb which fell right next to her tenement building, when the enemy were aiming for nearby Dixon's Blazes Ironworks, Clydebridge Steelworks and Clydesmill Power Station. It rocked the building and threw her out of bed but she was fortunate because part of the building was destroyed and several neighbours were killed.

On one of those nights when we had an air-raid warning around 2 am, we were told there was a low-flying aircraft approaching and it was probably trying to bomb the coal mines nearby. As on other occasions when the air-raid sirens sounded we went to the air-raid shelter on the edge of the back green. It was built of reinforced concrete including the floor and roof and was about the size of a single car garage. There was a small metal door but no window. Getting ten families in, including about sixteen children, was quite a squeeze. Having been wakened in the night we children were generally fractious but the adults tried to amuse us with stories or singing. After an anxious wait of an hour or so the all-clear siren sounded and we returned to our homes. We learned the following day that the low-flying aircraft was simply a barrage balloon that had broken free of its mooring and was floating over High Blantyre. Many areas nearby were bombed during the Blitz but we were fortunate that none of the buildings in our small area were hit.

Grandfather

My maternal grandmother died before I was born and my earliest memory of my grandfather is of him sitting on his armchair smoking his pipe. I really liked the smell of pipe smoke which gave me a feeling of security and contentment, and I remember thinking I would smoke a pipe when I was old enough. This was probably because both my grandfather and my favourite uncle, Uncle Tam, smoked the pipe. Fortunately I don't smoke; pipe or cigarettes. The only thing I ever smoked was a cinnamon stick as pretend smoking. My grandfather often set me on his knee and sang to me but the only thing I remember him singing was:

> *Ma auntie Kate fell ower the gate,*
> *Ten puddins oan a plate,*
> *Yin fell aff and yin fell oan,*
> *Weel done ma auntie Kate.*

Grandmother

My paternal grandfather died before my birth and my grandmother lived in a tenement flat on Main Street, High Blantyre. Her youngest daughter Aunt Maisie lived with her till her marriage in 1949. We visited Grandma and she us on occasions. They too had plots to provide food during the war and post-war years and Dad, in addition to tending ours, went to dig their plot and plant seeds.

Punishment

We had a loving and secure family life and I can only remember two occasions when I was physically hit by my parents. On both occasions it was because I refused to come in as it was getting dark in the evening. On the first occasion I was climbing up the railings on the outside staircase to the upper flats. My mother called me in but I didn't go so my father was sent out to get me. He pulled me off the railings, gave me a single slap on the back of my head and told me to get in. I was crying when I went in and this infuriated my mother, so that when I should have been getting a telling-off it was my father who was ticked off.

On the second occasion my sister Isabel was sent out to call me in and I hid in the air-raid shelter of an adjacent street till she went back in, by which time it was really dark. When I eventually went in my mother was sitting by the paraffin lamp darning socks. She had obviously been frantic with worry and was very angry with me so she got up and laid into me with the sock she had been darning; the proverbial marshmallow hitting a balloon. I was crying, not because it was painful but because my feelings were hurt—until my father came over and said, 'Stop it, you've hit him enough now.'

Clean Inside and Out

Bath-time was once a week when a tin bath was filled in front of the coal fire and we bathed one by one. Fleas and lice were occasional visitors and we had nightly checks for signs of the little pests. Any time we had head lice we had our heads washed and any nits loosened with vinegar. Then came the feared bone comb to remove the offending creatures. My hair was curly and having that fine-toothed comb pulled through it was an ordeal.

There was also a weekly ritual of making sure our bowels were moving regularly when we were given a dose of the dreaded castor oil. My mother gave it me with orange juice to try and mask the taste. This didn't work and only succeeded in putting me off oranges and orange juice for most of my childhood!

Medical Matters

When I was about six or seven there was an outbreak of scarlet fever and my sister Isabel caught it first. She was admitted to Motherwell Fever Hospital, later Strathclyde Hospital. While she was there I got it, and my admission to hospital was arranged. Our GP, Dr Gordon, was told I would have to go to another hospital much further out in Lanarkshire, making it impossible for our parents to visit both of us. He argued that this would be very cruel to our parents and they somehow found a bed for me at Motherwell Fever Hospital too. We were nursed in isolation in glass cubicles by *fever nurses*.

Scarlet fever is a highly infectious bacterial illness and spread rapidly in the overcrowded housing conditions which prevailed at that time, and this was before penicillin was available for general use. Parents were only allowed to visit once a week on a Sunday afternoon, but although they were not allowed to see us the visit was very important to them and to us. They could ask about our progress and bring small presents to hand in at the office. This was the highlight of the week to us. One of the presents I received was a writing set with pencil, paper and envelopes. I wrote a letter to Mum and Dad, and another to John in my childish writing. These were fumigated and handed over at visiting the following Sunday.

Isabel was in a different ward but when she was well enough to go home, the nurse brought her to the door of my cubicle and we were allowed to wave to each other through the glass. John was disappointed because he didn't get *the fever* and when the ambulance brought Isabel home he ran out very excitedly because he thought they'd come for him.

Following that I had frequent bouts of tonsillitis, and quinsy which is an abscess around the tonsil. Although penicillin was still not generally available, sulphonamide produced by May & Baker now was, and I had several courses of that to little benefit. I can remember my father saying to my mother once, 'There's no point going to the doctor again. He'll only give him more M&Bs.'

The doctor advised that my tonsils be removed. The homoeopath they had often consulted was very displeased, and gave them dire warnings of the dreadful and permanent damage chloroform would do to my internal organs. My paternal grandmother gave similar warnings. Happily my parents ignored the warnings and went ahead with the operation.

This was done by our family doctor after Sunday morning church service. Mum was instructed to open up the extending table and cover it with a sheet. Clean towels and boiling water were to be ready when he and his assistant arrived. On their arrival I was helped to climb up on the table and lie on my back. The assistant put a cloth over my nose and mouth and dripped chloroform on to it till I was out. Then Dr Gordon removed my tonsils. I recall waking up as I was being carried back to my bed. My throat was sore and I spat up blood for a few days afterwards but the bonus was frequent jelly and occasional ice cream. This was just before the introduction of the National Health Service so my parents had to pay for the operation.

Naturopathic treatments, which avoided any form of medication or surgery but concentrated on natural treatments such as diet, lots of fluid, fresh air and exercise, were preferred by my paternal grandmother and this influenced my father's attitude to medical treatments. My mother had a preference for homoeopathic or herbal treatments.

Before the inception of the NHS in 1948 a local homoeopath or herbalist was consulted for medical ailments because they charged less than the doctor, and if they failed to cure the problem, then the doctor was called in. After 1948 the doctor was consulted first since it was free, but if he failed to cure the problem the opinion of a homoeopath or herbalist would be sought.

My mother suffered from a lot of abdominal pain and most of the available treatments didn't help, but bicarbonate of soda (baking soda) did give short-term relief and she consumed a lot of it. Dr Gordon said this wasn't good for her kidneys, but no doctor, herbalist or homoeopath could help so he referred her to a specialist surgeon at Glasgow Royal Infirmary. He took a careful history, examined her and arranged X-rays then told her,

'You have a duodenal ulcer and the only effective treatment is an operation.' Mum wasn't happy at the prospect, but since she was experiencing a lot of pain, agreed. However on the way out she overheard a conversation between a nurse and a waiting patient.

The nurse said, 'We try to keep patients who need an operation away from that surgeon.'

This conversation was unethical and appeared to puzzle the patient, who asked, 'Why?'

'His success rate isn't good. In fact only about half of his patients survive the operation,' came the reply. Mum bolted as fast as her wee legs could carry her and never went back. It wasn't until the mid 1970s when Tagamet (cimetidine) was produced that she found a really effective treatment for her ulcer.

Isabel too had her share of medical problems. In addition to scarlet fever she later had rheumatic fever which made her very ill for months and left permanent damage to her heart valves. When she was about eight or nine she was noted to have a curvature of her spine and this slowly got worse. The GP thought it would settle in time and suggested exercises. My parents bought a device to hang over the door so that Isabel could swing on it to try to pull the spine straight, but it continued to worsen. When she was about fourteen Isabel was referred to an orthopaedic surgeon who stretched her to straighten the spine and then put her in a plaster jacket for several months. The condition was never cured but this appeared to produce some improvement and prevented further deterioration.

A Sick Cat

I had seen quite a lot of our family doctor before and after the inception of the NHS, and other alternative practitioners before then, partly because of my mother's constant quest to get relief from her ulcer pain and my father's six or seven episodes of pneumonia with pleurisy, but also because of my head injury, a broken arm playing football, frequent throat infections and scarlet fever. I was particularly impressed with Dr Gordon intervening to get my sister and me into the same hospital. In addition I had scalded my leg with hot tea resulting in a very large blister and he came regularly to dress it. I also had a spell of suffering from boils and carbuncles and had to attend the doctor regularly to have them lanced and the pus squeezed out of them. This was painful but cured me. On those occasions when the boils burst and didn't need to be lanced Mum would squeeze the boil herself and then, with Aunt Jenny's help, make up a paste with Epsom salts and glycerine and apply it. This was to 'draw' the pus. I saw her do the same with John when he had a boil.

All of this made me think I would like to be a doctor. I mentioned this to my parents but my mother said, 'People like us can't be doctors. We don't have the brains for that.'

My father came at it from a different angle and said, 'Don't try to get above your station in life, sir. Pride comes before a fall.'

47

The idea still simmered but I was given no encouragement. Then one day I was playing on the communal back green and saw a cat vomiting. I went into the house feeling sick and told my mother, who said, 'Well that's that; if you feel ill after seeing a sick cat there's no way you can be a doctor.' That put the idea out of my mind for a while but it continued to surface from time to time.

Chores

As children we each had our chores to do. When my mother was cooking I was often sent out to the *pig bin* with the peelings. These were collected by Jock Steen the piggery man a couple of times a week to feed his pigs. Nowadays when I put vegetable peelings in the kitchen bin I look back on those days and think, what a waste! Johnny the oil man came round once a week and we were sent out to his cart to get a week's supply of paraffin for the Aladdin lamp and the paraffin cooker.

On a Saturday morning we took the rugs out and hung them over the coal cellar wall to beat them with the handle of a cane walking stick. The two back doorsteps and shared porch of the two houses under the upstairs landing were scrubbed weekly with the two families responsible in turn. This was my job but in fact the other family never took their turn so I did it weekly. I must have made a good job of it because our neighbour was giving his daughter a telling-off one day and brought her out by the scruff of the neck to see my handiwork. He said, 'Do you see that? It was a boy who did that.' I think the implication was, boys shouldn't have to do that sort of thing but you're a girl and you should be doing it.

When I was old enough I had regular shopping to do. On Friday after walking home from school I was sent back up the same road to the grocery shop opposite the school with a *line* or list for the weekend's groceries. I recall being given a ten-shilling note, quite a lot then but only 50p in decimal currency, and the ration book since food was not only priced in money but also in coupons.

Having to walk all the way back to school after coming home was always a bit of a chore. As a very religious family we were taught to pray, not only before going to bed at night but at any time and in any place when we wanted to speak to God. Because we closed our eyes to say our prayers at night and when we said The Lord's Prayer in school, I thought it was essential to close my eyes if I wanted to pray. One Friday as I was walking home from school, Mum and Isabel were looking out of the window. Mum said to Isabel, 'Look, oor James is walking down the road with his eyes shut. I bet he's praying that he won't need to go back up the road to the shop. Ouch!' That is exactly what I was doing and I had just walked into a lamp post. But God didn't answer my prayer as I wanted. I was sent back up the road, lump on forehead and all.

Another regular weekend job was going to Jimmy Sweeney the butcher to get meat for the weekend. We stood in the queue on the sawdust-covered floor with the wall lined with carcasses; cows, sheep, pigs and poultry. Heads, skins and internal organs had been removed but it was clear to all what they were. The first time he asked me my name I said 'James,' because that was what my mother called me.

He replied, 'James is a horse's name, Jimmy's much better,' and I preferred Jimmy from then on. My pals all called me Jimmy but my father's sister, Aunt Maisie, always called me Jim but in a very affected sort of way that made it sound like *Jeem*. I hated that and disliked being called Jim for a long time because of it. Mum continued to call me James.

Most parents sent their children to the shops for odds and ends. On one occasion just after my twelfth birthday when I was playing with Tommy O'Neill from the front of the building, Mrs O'Neill came out and called Tommy. Realising this probably meant a chore he ran off so Mrs O'Neill called me and I responded. She gave me two shillings and asked me to go the chemist in High Blantyre Main Street to buy Epsom salts and glycerine because her husband had a boil.

In those days a visit to the chemist took a long time because they had to make up almost all medicines by hand in the back shop. Reluctantly I agreed and went off to the chemist. When my turn came I said, 'A packet of Epsom salts and a bottle of glycerine please.'

He replied, 'Do you not mean Epsom-salts-and-glycerine paste?'

'No,' I said, 'they must be separate.' I had seen Mum make up a paste and apply it to a carbuncle I had on my neck and to a boil John had.

When I arrived at the door and proudly presented Mrs O'Neill with my purchases she looked shocked and said, 'That's no good to me, I need Epsom-salts-and-glycerine paste.'

Reluctant to go all the way back to the shop and admit to making a mistake I replied, 'But Mum mixes it herself, and I know how to do it.'

'I don't,' she answered, 'but if you know how, you come in and do it for me.' As I started walking into the house she continued, 'Do you know how to put it on a boil?'

'Yes, I've had it put on my carbuncles and I've seen it put on John's boil.' By this time I was inside their home, a single end like ours.

After mixing the ingredients into a paste, I watched as she applied the paste to white lint, and was about to put it on her husband's boil, which was leaking pus. Remembering the pain of having my carbuncles squeezed I said, 'I think you need to squeeze the poison out first.' I knew Mrs O'Neill better than most of the adults in our area because we both did some casual work on the farm and often worked together so I felt able to speak to her more freely than I usually would.

'I can't do that,' she replied, 'but seeing you know so much you squeeze it.' Her husband was looking decidedly anxious by this time. The idea of a twelve-year-old squeezing his already painful boil was alarming but he agreed. I had never squeezed a boil before but I'd had it done to me on several occasions and knew it hurt, but I had a go using two wads of cotton wool. Lots of smelly pus came out and Mr O'Neill was cursing me. After this I applied the lint and paste and Mrs O'Neill secured it with sticky tape. Mr O'Neill grunted a thank you to me afterwards and muttered something about it feeling better.

Feeling self-satisfied, I went home and told Mum what I had done. I said, 'I didn't feel sick the way I was with the cat; I can be a doctor.'

She said, 'I can do that but it doesn't make me a doctor, and it doesn't make you one either.'

Although these were regular chores for us children, one occasional visitor to the tenement was a real headache for Mum, and all mothers. He was the ragman who came with a cart calling, 'Toys for rags.' We all pestered our mothers for old clothes to get some of the treasure, usually balloons, peashooters, chalk or other trinkets. The following poem by an anonymous poet paints the scene well.

The Ragman

He gave you fair warning whenever he came
Though the tune he played was never the same.
In a neighbouring street a bugler played,
And it wasn't the Lifeboys or Boys' Brigade.

All the young mothers were gripped with fear
As this dreaded bugler came ever near.
'Tis the ragman playing a chordless tune,
The bedraggled Pied Piper of Glesga toon.

Came into our street pushing his cart,
Blowing his bugle right from the start.
His old brown case was full of toys
Like Santa's grotto to the girls and boys.

Paint sets and crayons and coloured chalk
To create a design on your whipping top,
Spud guns and peashooters and catapult slings,
The toys of war the ragman brings

Took out a Woodbine, the last of his fags,
Then he bellowed, 'Toys for rags.'
Last blast on the bugle and then he'd hush,
Lit up and waited for the expected rush.

The kids in the street would all go mad,
Looking for rags from their mum and dad,
In all the cupboards throughout the room,
A handful of rags for a coloured balloon.

With great anticipation they stood in line,
Eyes fixed on the ragman all of the time.
No pounds and ounces of imperial measure,
Just a bundle of rags for unlimited treasure.

Though I could only stand and stare,
We never seemed to have rags to spare.
Now looking back and assessing the facts,
All of our rags were on our backs.

Anon

We had a number of Roman Catholic neighbours and they weren't allowed to eat meat on a Friday, I think as a sort of self-sacrifice in recognition of Jesus' death on the cross on Good Friday. They usually ate fish. We had a fish van come round twice a week, on a Tuesday and Friday, and most Protestants bought their fish on the Tuesday in case somebody saw them and thought they were Catholics. But my mother always made a point of buying her fish on a Friday because, she said, 'The fish man sells more fish on a Friday because of the Catholics and so it's very fresh.' She always bought filleted haddock but had a dreadful fear of fish bones and didn't trust the fishmonger's filleting, so she went over it again thoroughly to make sure there wasn't a single bone. I don't know if it's genetic or learned behaviour but I have the same fear of fish bones.

Christianity

Sundays in our Sabbatarian household could be a bit boring. We weren't allowed out to play but we did enjoy going to Sunday school. When we were quite small we went to High Blantyre Baptist Church, also known as The Wee Tin Church. It was quite near and had been my mother's church before she married my father. I have happy memories of sitting there singing choruses such as:

Running over, running over
My cup's full and running over,
Since the Lord saved me,
I'm as happy as can be
My cup's full and running over.

Image 2-5: High Blantyre Baptist Church (Wattie's
Wee Tin Kirk). Wattie and Tina Wilson inset.
Courtesy of High Blantyre Baptist Church

My parents were members of the Christian Brethren who had moved to Bethany Hall, Glasgow Road in Low Blantyre, and when we were older we walked there to Sunday school and to the weekly children's meeting on a Wednesday evening. This was the highlight of the week.

It was before the days of television, let alone computer games, but my father would not allow even a radio in the house, and since we weren't allowed to go to the cinema these services were our entertainment with lots of singing and actions. Speakers often brought flannel-graphs to illustrate Bible stories, or occasionally slides for the magic lantern. This was usually a series of slides telling a story with a moral lesson. Since most evangelical churches were aligned to the temperance movement they often showed the evils of drink or gambling. Sometimes they would be about the exploits of foreign missionaries or illustrate a Bible story.

Image 2-6: Former Bethany Hall, now a nursery.

On Sunday evenings after the evening service my parents usually had a few people from the church back for supper. After the meal the adults all gathered round the organ and had a sing-song. My father and Isabel played by ear. Needless to say it was all hymns they sang and sometimes children's choruses but it was an enjoyable end to the day.

My pals and I joined the Boy Scouts when old enough. I enjoyed that—but only for one session; then my father objected and I had to stop going. One of his reasons was that it coincided with the weekly children's meeting in Bethany Hall and I should be taking my friends there, to try to get them 'converted', rather than me going with them. But he had another reason. He was strongly anti-military and believed that with the drills, the marching, the salutes, the Scout promise and especially the parade on Remembrance Sunday, the movement was designed to encourage us to join the armed forces when old enough.

Living in a tenement, and especially one near a farm, our homes were frequently visited by furry friends, usually mice but there was an occasional rat. Mousetraps were an essential part of our household equipment and were set by our parents before they went to bed at night.

Once a year the Sunday school held a soirée. It was a Christian concert where the children did turns and the parents came along. My father wrote a poem for my brother John to recite when he was about nine years old. I have reproduced it in an Anglicised version below. It epitomises his attitude to worldly pleasures, and also that of evangelical churches in general, such as Baptists, Pentecostals, Nazarenes and the Brethren at that time. The version in the Blantyre dialect can be viewed on my website: www.ascottishdoctor.com/home-family

The Trap

My mother bought a brand new trap
To catch that rascal mouse.
It's such a cheeky little chap
You'd think it owned the house.

A piece of cheese just toasted brown,
Temptation on a spring.
A tasty little snack laid down
To catch the crafty thing.

Going to bed we set about
And soon were fast asleep,
Then through a hole the mouse came out
And carefully did creep.

Towards the trap it turned its head,
And moved near to the cheese.
Then 'SNAP,' we heard, the mouse was dead,
Allured to death with ease.

Of Satan's plans I now must tell.
He sets his traps for us,
To try to lure us down to Hell
With pleasures numerous.

Attractions of the world we find,
In dancing and football,
And cinema to fill the mind,
So I must tell you all,

'Love not the world,' the Bible says,
Repent, Christ will forgive,
For by His blood our souls He saves.
Trust now in Him and live.
John Graham c.1951 & James Graham 2011

One of the practical benefits of belonging to a church was the care and concern shown to each other in times of difficulty. I mentioned my father's numerous episodes of pneumonia and pleurisy. Before we had penicillin this was a life-threatening illness and involved a prolonged period of being unable to work. Even with penicillin he was still unable to work for two or three weeks. This time off work brought considerable hardship since there was no sick pay. Before the introduction of the Welfare State, members of the church visited regularly, and on leaving would hand some money to Mum, depending on their ability to give.

With the introduction of the Welfare State and of Sickness Benefit, things were not quite so difficult but still not good. I recall just after 1948 when Dad was ill again he still had visitors from the church, but not as many as before. Most still gave some money but not as much as before. Some, however, stopped giving and I overheard one couple who had been visiting. As they left they shook hands with Mum and instead of slipping her a few shillings they said, 'You won't be needing any money from us now that you have this Sickness Benefit.'

My Father

My father was a good man and worked hard to keep his family. He never ill-treated us in any way but he tended to be distant and rather gruff. Spending time with his children was considered frivolous compared with the

Image 2-7: My father preaching in the street supported by some reluctant looking friends.

high calling of preaching the gospel. I treasure the memory of the very few times he did play with us but they were always in response to pressure from my mother. Having left home at 4 am to go to work he would come home around 3 or 3.30 pm, have a meal, sleep on the chair for half an hour, and then wash, change and go out to preach.

He was a remnant of a time when there were back-court entertainers. His contribution to this 'entertainment' was to go to back courts of tenements, sing a gospel hymn, and preach the Christian Gospel.

James Cornfield, using the language and imagery of the day, captures the scene very well in this excerpt from his poem *You Can't Take The Man Out Of The Street*:

The street was busy in those far off days,
People from all over came our way,
Blin' Watty, Cheap Johnny, the Old Co-op van,
Alex Kerr the shilling-a-week man,
Wee Dom the Tally, the Ice Cream man,
Johnny the Darkie with case in hand
Jenny the Pack, the Provident man,
***Mr John Graham** the Preacher man.*

Wullie Tonner, mouthpiece and clappers,
Playing tunes that drove us crackers,
A Blin' man who sang like a Linnet,
Then sent his pal round with the Bunnet,
Strooling Minstrels from all the Airts,
Men selling fruit from open Cairts,
They all sang for their daily bread,
Any song for a Penny could be heard.[4]

James Cornfield 2005

---

[4] *You Can't Take The Man Out Of The Street,* James Cornfield 2005, Changing Places published by *Changing Places Blantyre*. Mr John Graham (my father), bold type mine.

The difference was that Mr John Graham the preacher man didn't do it for pennies but in the hope that some would listen and that, occasionally, someone might get converted. His preaching continued daily, long after most tenements and back-court entertainers had disappeared. He usually undertook this on his own, mainly because others were not willing to stand and preach in this way, but he did have one friend from Rutherglen, Frank George, who shared his passion for this kind of preaching. Uncle Frank, as we children knew him, often came to Blantyre and supported my father, who sometimes went to Rutherglen to support him. In addition the local Brethren Church held an open air meeting on a Sunday evening before the main service and he as well as others participated in that.

Although learning a trade was the pinnacle of his ambition for my brother John and me, he did have ambitions for his sons to be lay preachers like himself. He was happy to interact with us when it involved spreading the Gospel. Training for this type of preaching didn't involve any form of higher education. It involved reading the Bible and other Christian books and then getting out and practising the preaching. Shortly after I started my bricklaying apprenticeship he persuaded one of my friends and me to go out with him and do some of the preaching. This didn't last very long because we both decided it wasn't for us.

My parents would have had ambitions for Isabel in-volving some form of training for office work such as shorthand and typing, but unfortunately her health problems resulted in her having very little secondary education and she was seventeen before she was fit for light work.

Notwithstanding my father's obsession with preaching, and his apparent lack of significant interaction with his children, we had a happy and secure home life and he was very much a part of that.

His friend Frank George emigrated to Canada around 1948 and wrote to my father suggesting he go there too. I remember overhearing a discussion between my parents when my father suggested he could go first and get a job, and then send for us. It was the first, and I think the only time when that feeling of security was shattered. He was always around, going to work, coming home from work, sleeping on the chair, going out to preach, coming home again and going to bed early, kneeling at his bed in prayer before getting into bed. Suddenly I didn't feel secure any more. Fortunately it didn't last for long. My mother made it absolutely clear we were not going to Canada and that was that. Blantyre was her home and in Blantyre she would remain.

During my last two or three years at primary school there was a lot of new council-house building going on and families in the overcrowded tenements were applying for the new houses. Homes and families were assessed and prioritised based on the state of their current buildings and levels of overcrowding. My understanding is that the local councillors had a lot of say in who got the houses, or at least that was the impression they liked to give.

Our local councillor, Jimmy Beecroft, had earned a good reputation for fighting for the rights of the poor in Blantyre but during this housing boom he also developed a liking for alcohol. In the pubs he would be plied with drink by men trying to influence him to get their families new houses. He gladly accepted their offers with promises to use his influence on their behalf, but he rarely did. My father met him in the street one day after Jimmy had been drinking and asked him if he could help our family, without any offer of drink.

He said, 'Aye, John, I'll try, but you know we are the two fools of Blantyre.'

My father answered, 'Aye Jimmy, that's true, I'm a fool for Christ's sake but whose fool are you?' This angered Jimmy and he swung a right hook giving Dad a black eye and bloody nose. I don't think he turned the other cheek; he simply walked away to avoid inflaming the situation.

My father did have other interests. He enjoyed, and was very good at, DIY although that was probably more through necessity than pleasure. When we were in the single end in High Blantyre he went to night classes with a friend from Bethany Hall, Jimmy Black. They did cabinet-making one year and he made a chest of drawers which was quite impressive even if the drawers did tend to stick a little. The following year they went to French polishing classes and he French-polished the chest of drawers. It looked really good.

There was one area where my father did interact with us and that was in connection with the Brethren

Church. The poem I quoted earlier was one example. He wrote poems for us to recite at the soirée every year.

Another example was making sure we were ready to get to church on time on a Sunday morning. Because he rose from bed at 3.30 am six days a week, having a lie-in was getting up around 7 am. His regular breakfast was orange and banana with brown bread, but on a Sunday he had fried bacon and egg. When we were teenagers and reluctant to get out of bed to go to church, he cooked bacon and eggs for us and gave us breakfast in bed. Then he made sure we didn't go back to sleep but got up and dressed on time. The other Sunday morning thing he did for us as teenagers was to clean our shoes so that we would be respectable going to church.

My Mother

What can I say of my mother that most people don't say about their mothers? It is fair to say that my father lived the Christian life. He was honest and morally upright and from time to time did acts of kindness such as giving money to someone in need, but his passion in life was preaching. If my father specialised in preaching the Christian gospel, my mother specialised in living the Christian life, or as some would say, 'He preached Christ but his wife lived Christ.' She demonstrated the love and compassion of Jesus in every aspect of her life. This didn't mean that she was in any way ashamed of her faith and she did speak to people about Jesus as the opportunity arose.

The difference of emphasis in their lives is illustrated very nicely by an incident that occurred one day shortly after we had moved to a council house in Cowan Wilson Avenue. This was a time when many Pakistani

Image 2-8: My mother. She hated having her photo taken so there are none of her when younger.

immigrants had come into the country and some of them went round knocking on doors with a case in hand trying to sell things. It was a cold winter's day and starting to snow.

A young Pakistani man appeared at the door with his case and asked my mother to buy something. He was miserable-looking and shivering in our cold Scottish weather. My mother did buy something; something she probably didn't need, and then invited him into the house and gave him a seat beside the coal fire. She gave him some hot soup, a hot drink and something to eat. She asked no questions about race or religion but simply showed an act of Christian kindness.

My father arrived home about this time and immediately asked the man if he was going to heaven. This was a common approach of my father when taking the opportunity to preach to people one-to-one. He started to tell the young man about his view of God and the need for faith in Christ. The young man said he was a Muslim and believed in Allah, and left.

My mother never turned a beggar away and I do remember many occasions when we were in the tenement in High Blantyre and she would put a little card table out at the back door under the upstairs landing and give them tea and sandwiches.

She also had a number of visitors who most people wouldn't allow in their homes. One regular was a woman called Sadie who was, for want of a better description, a low-grade prostitute. Sadie had poor personal hygiene and what was then known as chronic bronchitis with a persistent moist cough. She charged her clients half a crown, 12½p in decimal money, and took them to a secluded, wooded area near the River Calder.

My mother never turned her or anyone else away but the routine was usually much the same; she brought out the little card table with a white tablecloth and gave them tea and food and chatted to them about life in general, listening to their many problems in life. She often tried to persuade Sadie to turn from her ways and spoke to her about Jesus and forgiveness, praying with her. Sadie usually promised to give up her lifestyle with her customary phrase, 'Aye, Maggie, aye, ah will,' only to return the following week to confess she hadn't been able to keep her promise.

Another occasional visitor was an elderly lady called Kate Cox who was a servant in Bardykes House. Her master and mistress were themselves elderly and very demanding. Kate was unmarried and had always been in service so had no home of her own. It was very comforting for her to be able to visit a proper home on her only half-day off. She suffered terribly from chilblains in the winter time but she found it rather difficult to get down to her own feet because of arthritis. My mother regularly applied Snowfire to Kate's feet. Snowfire is a thick type of green ointment which is very soothing on chilblains.

Sunday papers were not allowed in our home but Aunt Jean used to cut out *Oor Wullie* and *The Broons* from the *Sunday Post* and send them to us regularly. My mother had two weekly magazines. One was *The Weekly News* which came out on a Thursday and featured one of my favourite cartoons, *Black Bob*, which was about the adventures of a sheepdog. The other was the *Christian Herald* which had a children's section and a children's club, the *Golden Star Brigade,* whose members were called 'cousins'. Often when children joined they would write about something they had done or quote a favourite children's hymn or poem, so I wrote my own Christian verse:

The Bible
There is news, wonderful news
In the Book which you should use.
It tells of Jesus Christ,
Who died to pay sin's price,
To make heav'n free
For you and me.

Several weeks later a girl was joining and quoted my poem as being her favourite. The editor commented that the verse had been written by an eleven-year-old cousin. My mother was very proud of this and kept the cutting for all of her life.

The attributes of a true Christian are listed in the Bible as the fruit of the Spirit, and my mother had them in abundance as I tried to show in my poem.

My Christian Mother
A sincere Christian was my mother,
As shown in her life ev'ry day.
Teaching us to love one another,
By loving she showed us the way.

Though her life was oft' filled with sadness,
And the road sometimes long and hard,
She displayed a God given calmness,
Joy and peace through trust in her Lord.

To others she was really kind
With gentleness and self-control.
Compassionate thoughts filled her mind,
Like Jesus, to help and console.

Her faithfulness to God above
Displayed the beauty of our Lord.
Her many selfless acts of love
Have surely brought her His reward.

Throughout her life my mother showed
The fruit of the Spirit of God.
From her the Living Water flowed,
Spreading the love of Christ abroad.

Books

I don't remember any pressure from my parents to work hard and achieve at school. To them, people like us didn't go into the professions or occupations requiring high educational standards, but fear of the teachers made us do our homework. However our parents did encourage us to learn in general and in addition to books of Bible stories they bought a set of encyclopaedia for us. It was, I think, *The Children's Encyclopaedia of Knowl-*

edge and in six volumes. Inside the cover of each volume were four lines from Rudyard Kipling's famous poem from *The Elephant's Child:*

> *I keep six honest serving men*
> *(They taught me all I knew);*
> *Their names are What and Why and When*
> *And How and Where and Who.*

These four lines made a big impression on me and encouraged me to think and ask questions. In addition my father's elderly uncle, Uncle Willie, who lived in Langholm in the Scottish Borders often sent us books of knowledge for birthdays or Christmas. They were usually heavily illustrated which made them more interesting, and two in particular I remember when I was twelve years of age. They were mainly composed of photographs. One was *Six Years of War in Pictures* and contained many graphic images from the Second World War.

The other contained all kinds of photographs and the one that stood out was a full frontal naked lady, simply entitled 'Nude'. I am surprised my parents made no effort to censor it, but in retrospect since there was never any discussion about the facts of life, I suppose it was a step in that direction. Another source of this kind of information was the *Family Doctor*, a book that was consulted for medical advice by most families, especially before the NHS when medical treatment had to be paid for. These *Family Doctor* books with their vivid illustrations not only gave information on diseases but also anatomy. They were regularly consulted by the adolescents in most households and ours was no exception.

Another book was a Christmas present from Grandma. It was *Black Beauty* and it made a great impression on me, creating a love and respect for horses. I loved watching the farm horses at work in the fields beside our tenement.

Chapter 3

Primary School Days

High Blantyre Primary School

High Blantyre Primary School was my first school. It was about half a mile from home and we all walked there.

Image 3-1: Primary 7 High Blantyre Primary School 1949.

In image 3-1, I am the tallest boy in the middle of the back row and the teacher on the left of the back row was the regular Primary 7 teacher, Mr Ferrier, generally known as Big Tam. As I recall he never used the belt. He didn't need to. He had an artificial arm and he made very effective use of that with a judicious clout to the back of the head or to push us into line.

Big Tam and a rather small female teacher, Miss Easton, lived about two miles from the school and they always walked there and back. The reason for this, he said, was that if we don't use our legs enough they'll get shorter and shorter in successive generations until eventually humans will lose their legs altogether. I don't know if he believed this but it draws its influence from a theory of evolution by a French biologist, Jean-Baptiste Lamarck, first published around 1801. This theory was of course superseded by Charles Darwin's theory of evolution by natural selection, first published in 1859.

The primary education we received there was good and prepared us well for secondary school. Life in school was fairly uneventful and I don't recall any incidents of bullying although there were a few occasions in Primary 6 or 7 when there was a fight between two boys. Fortunately I was never involved in any fights at primary school, although I did once get in a fight with a boy who went to a different school. I don't think any blows were struck. We seemed to do a lot of sparring with his pals shouting, 'Come on, Frankie,' and my pals shouting, 'Come on, Jimmy.' It ended when a couple of men came down the road and told us to go home.

Food was in short supply during the war years and as mentioned we had ration books for food and clothing. However food parcels were sent, from Canada I think, and were distributed in school. In the autumn we were instructed to go out to the hedgerows and collect rose hips which we handed in at school. They were sent off to make rose-hip syrup, a very good source of vitamin C.

We learned the rudiments of poetry in Primary 6 or 7 which I enjoyed. The local primary schools held a Burns Night competition and I was put forward to represent our school when I was in Primary 7. I recited a poem, not by Robert Burns, but by another more recent Scottish poet, John M. Caie. The poem is entitled *The Puddock* and I won second prize in the competition. The theme is 'pride comes before a fall' and it has been my favourite poem since then. The old Scottish dialect can be difficult for those not familiar with it, including modern Scots, so I've included an Anglicised version below.

The Puddock

A puddock sat by the lochan's brim,
An' he thocht there was never a puddock like him.
He sat on his hurdies, he waggled his legs,
An' cockit his heid as he glowered throu' the seggs.
The bigsy wee cratur' was feelin' that prood,
He gapit his moo' an' he croakit oot lood:
"Gin ye'd a' like tae see a richt puddock," quo' he,
"Ye'll never, I'll sweer, get a better nor me.
I've fem'lies an' wives an' a weel plenished hame,
Wi' drink for my thrapple an' meat for my wame.
The lassies aye thocht me a fine strappin' chiel,
An' I ken I'm a rael bonny singer as weel.
I'm nae gon tae blaw, but th' truth I maun tell
I believe I'm the verra MacPuddock himsel'."

A heron was hungry an' needin' tae sup,
Sae he nabbit th' puddock and gollup't him up;
Syne runkled his feathers: "A peer thing," quo' he,
"But puddocks is nae fat they eesed tae be."

The Frog
A frog sat by the edge of the pond,
And he thought there was never a frog like him.
He sat on his buttocks, he shook his legs,
And tilted his head as he stared through the irises.
The arrogant little creature was feeling so proud,
He opened his mouth and he croaked out loud:
"If you'd all like to see a real frog," said he,
"You'll never, I'll swear, get better than me.
I've families and wives and a well-furnished home,
With drink for my throat and food for my stomach.
The girls always thought me a fine strapping lad,
And I know I'm a really nice singer as well.
I'm not going to boast, but the truth I must tell
I believe I'm the Frog Clan chieftain himself."

A heron was hungry and needing to eat,
So he grabbed the frog and swallowed him quickly.
Then wrinkled his feathers: "A poor thing," said he,
"But frogs are not what they used to be."

Play

There was plenty of room outside for play when not at school. We had the back courts of the three tenements, three fields belonging to the farm, Broompark Road itself which had very little traffic and we had the banking of the railway line which only had two or three slow moving goods trains per week.

Most of my friends who were in my class at school had better toys than I owned, for example superior roller skates and a scooter with ball bearings in the wheels. My roller skates and scooter didn't have ball bearings so I was much slower than they were. When the snow came two of my closest friends, John Robertson and Billy McPhee had sledges, which I never had. Their fathers worked in engineering and made the sledges for them at work. John and Billy were never selfish with them and we all had equal turns, either on a sloping pavement nearby or on the *pit bing* or pit heap 300 yards down the road.

I often went with my parents to visit Aunt Jenny Scott. She lived in a tenement in Low Blantyre and I thought they were rich because they had a room and a kitchen. They also had hole-in-the-wall beds and I used to crawl under one, because stored beneath was a bike that had belonged to my older cousin. He was much older than I and had outgrown the bike years earlier. Oh how I wished it could be mine!

It was given to me eventually when I was a little too big for it, and then I had something none of my pals had at that time. My sister, Isabel, who was three years older, helped me to balance on it and then she learned to ride, although she too was a bit too big for it. Then all our friends came round to learn *to go the bike*. My brother, John, was four years younger and too small to reach the pedals but he also learned to balance on it.

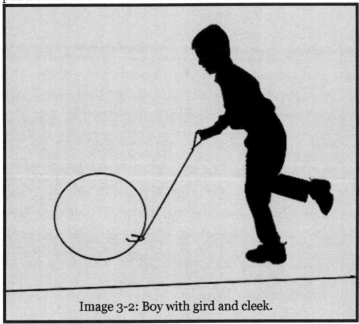

Image 3-2: Boy with gird and cleek.

In addition to playing the usual cops and robbers or cowboys and Indians we had *girds and cleeks* which we ran for miles with. A gird is a circle of mild steel of eighteen inches to two feet in diameter. The cleek is a metal rod with a hook on the end and was used to push the gird along. They were not unique to Scotland but were known by different names in different parts of the UK. Hoop and stick was a designation used in some areas. In industrial Britain they were made by black-smiths, shipbuilders and engineers as children's toys. There was a blacksmith further down Broompark Road and he made girds and cleeks. I bought one with my pocket money.

Although *beds or peever* was a girls' game the boys sometimes played too. Beds were a series of squares drawn on the pavement and the peever was a flat stone or old shoe polish tin. The game was known as hopscotch in many parts of the country. We hopped across the squares pushing the peever but had to prevent it or our feet touching the lines. Skipping ropes were used to run with in much the same way as with the girds and cleeks. But skipping with one person at either end of the rope and others jumping in was for the girls. Although we considered that kind of skipping to be cissy, the fact was the girls were much more skilled with ropes than the boys. Hide and seek, *bools* or marbles and *buttony*, like tiddlywinks but using buttons, were also played.

Those of us who were in the same class at school played well together with very little friction or fallouts but occasionally older boys from further afield came to our area and they often tried to bully us. Fortunately this mainly occurred in the frost when we had slides on the sloping pavement. Because they didn't have a suitable slope in their area they tried to take control of ours. This didn't last for long though, because the people living in the semi-detached houses adjacent usually came out and put salt down to melt the ice. We had other alternatives, the pit bing 300 yards down the road being a favourite.

Rockhead's Farm

There were many children in the area but four of us, John, Bill, Pete and I, formed a closer bond. When we were older, perhaps from about age ten, the four of us went to Rockhead's farm a lot. This was just on the other side of the railway line and we were allowed to play around the farm whenever we wanted because we did some small jobs such as helping with the milking (by hand on a three-legged stool), mucking the byre, helping build hayricks at harvest time, and *tatie howkin* or helping to take cattle to new pastures. Twice a year we would take young cattle to or from Achentibber above High Blantyre, a distance of about one mile, where they pastured during the summer months.

The milking cattle were kept in the byre over the winter and let out in spring. It was a real joy to see them running, jumping and skipping like spring lambs as we took them the 300 yards along the road to the field just in front of our window. Twice daily they had the trip back to the farm for milking. Occasionally an animal would be taken to the slaughterhouse and we were allowed to go along to watch. Looking back I would have thought as an eleven-year-old this should upset me but it didn't. This may have been because of my shopping trips to Jimmy Sweeney the butcher where I brushed against all sorts of animal carcasses hanging in the front shop. The animal to be slaughtered was put in a stall and the slaughter man walked up and calmly shot it in the forehead. The animal then fell to the floor. I thought that was it dead but now I know it was only stunned and the killing was done by slitting its throat. I didn't see that bit. Trips on the tractor trailer taking grain to a mill in Hamilton were highlights because it seemed so far away and it was interesting watching the watermill in action.

The farm was run by old Jimmy Rockhead and two of his sons Arthur and Bob and their sister Maisie. There was a yearly agricultural show in East Kilbride and Arthur, who was in his early thirties and the youngest of the three Rockhead sons, took us there. As well as seeing horses and cattle judged, there were tractor-driving and ploughing competitions and then a gymkhana and motorcycle speedway racing. It was for us a really exciting day out.

Once a year we saw the steam traction engine, with the threshing machine in tow, chugging up Broompark Road to the farm and we knew it was threshing time. The big flywheel on the traction engine drove the threshing machine and this was loaded using a horse-drawn contraption that lifted the corn and dropped it into the machine. We helped in ways such as lifting the straw or corn, but most of all by helping the farm dogs and cats to kill the mice and rats that had been nesting in the corn. The cats, in particular, were efficient hunters. They would catch a mouse and then play with it by throwing it in the air to catch again. Our job was to club the mouse with a heavy stick to kill it, thus encouraging the cat to get another. We also ran after mice independently of the cats to kill them with our sticks. Did I feel sorry for the animals I was killing? I did, and I certainly didn't enjoy that aspect of farm work. Unfortunately such sentiments had to be set aside during threshing at Broompark Farm. As many as possible of the little creatures had to be killed to stop them eating the grain.

I helped with milk deliveries at the weekend. This was delivered from large milk urns on the back of a

Image 3-3: Tippin cairt with life-sized model horse at Rosebank Garden Centre in the Clyde valley.

horse-drawn cart and taken to the customers in an open milk can. We also went out to deliver potatoes, vegetables or garden manure on a two-wheeled cart known as a *tippin cairt*.

On one occasion my friend John and I were helping deliver manure to some of the local houses with gardens. We used a fork to push the smelly substance on to the side of the road in neat piles. John and I were standing at the back of the cart, which was slippy with the remnants of the manure on the return journey, when we came up to Granny Clark's house. Granny Clark was a devout Catholic whose favourite saint was St Francis. She threw bread on the road to feed the birds in the hope of his interceding for her. Our horse decided this was too good an opportunity to miss and bent down to eat some bread. As he went down the front of the cart went down with him, jerking the back upwards, and I was thrown over the back, landing on my head. I was rendered unconscious and have no recollection of the actual accident. I just remember gaining consciousness momentarily as I was being carried into our tenement back court towards the house. The doctor came to examine me and my parents were warned of signs of serious damage to watch for. No permanent harm resulted but I was banned from the farm for a few weeks.

Pulling power on the farm was supplied by two horses and two tractors. They were two very different horses. One was a big Clydesdale, Harry; a placid animal and a joy to be around. He pulled the heavier loads such as implements for ground preparation like harrowing. Dick was the other, lighter cart horse; he was more temperamental and we were always warned not to go too near. Bob Rockhead had a permanent limp due to a fracture sustained a few years earlier when Dick kicked him. Dick pulled the milk cart and other lighter loads.

I remember my father talking of the days when he had a two-horse team pulling his bread van. One was a very willing worker and pulled hard but the other was lazy and let the other take the strain. He often used this in his preaching when speaking of the need for all pulling together.

Sometimes for heavy work such as ploughing or drilling, the two horses, heavy Harry and lighter Dick, were yoked together. It looked odd and I'm sure Harry took the heavier load but they did manage to do the job fairly well.

The two tractors gradually replaced the horses for field work. One was an old green Fordson Major with broad mudguards and a seat at the end of a steel bar. This gave it a superb spring effect and old Jimmy Rockhead loved that. We sat on the mudguards on the way to and from the fields. It had a temperamental engine which they appeared to spend a lot of time tinkering with. Later they acquired a smaller, lighter, grey Ferguson that was much faster. Old Jimmy hated it because it didn't have the springy seat of the Fordson. It often got stuck in the mud and needed the Fordson to pull it out.

John and I had our pet animals at the farm. John's was a heifer we called Bambie and mine a bullock we named Totie. Since he was my favourite sometimes I would crawl through a hole in the hedge in front of our window to go into the field to see him. Occasionally he followed me back through the hole to my back door. It was not an easy job getting him back into the field.

I loved being among the animals and we learned a lot. The bull was not put in the field with cows but we were asked to keep our eyes open for cows coming into season. They referred to it as being *a-bullin*. One cow would mount the other and if it didn't resist it was receptive, so we informed the farmer. The cow was taken to the farmyard on a halter and the bull brought out of his shed to perform his duty. There was one occasion when Mum and I were at the window which overlooked the field and we saw a cow mounting another.

I said, 'Look, that cow's a-bullin, I need to go and tell Arthur.' I knew exactly what that meant since I had watched the procedure many times in the farm. Perhaps my mother was too embarrassed to discuss it further since she changed the subject. I'm not sure who was supposed to teach whom about the birds and bees, not to mention cows, bulls and humans.

In due course new calves were born and this was an interesting adventure, especially if there was a problem and the vet had to be called. The thought of being a vet occurred to me but that received the same response from my parents as the suggestion I might be a doctor.

Old Jimmy Rockhead's third son, James, had his own farm at Millheugh. This was also in Blantyre but on the other side of the River Calder, and we sometimes went there to help out at harvest time. I think I must have been accident-prone because once, when standing on the back of the float carrying a hayrick to the farm, I put my hand up to pull off a small branch as we passed under a tree. The branch was stronger than I thought and pulled me off, making me do a somersault in the process. There were some bruises, but no significant injuries.

I recently watched a TV programme showing the sophisticated methods of sowing seeds nowadays. The tractor was guided by GPS and computerised messages between the tractor and seed-spreader adjusted the distribution of the seed. What a contrast with methods then!

When we went to the farm there was a mechanised seed-spreader but it was quite light and only worked properly if we sat on it to add weight. There was one occasion when it was quite cold with some drizzle and I put on my new raincoat. The tail end of the coat became caught up in the sprockets spreading the seed and was pulled in, tearing in the process. Bob was driving the tractor and didn't hear me shouting, 'Woah, Boab, woah.' Meanwhile my coat was being drawn further into the machinery. Eventually when the three of us, John, Billy and I, shouted at the same time he did hear us and stopped. He reversed the tractor and seed-spreader and I was able to slowly pull my coat tail out. I was scared to tell Mum and hid the coat but obviously it couldn't remain a secret for long. A telling-off was delivered and she did manage to do a reasonable repair on it, so that was that.

Looking back to my younger days before that level of mechanisation, I remember old Jimmy sowing seed in one of the fields beside the building. He walked up and down the field with a large flat tray in front of him, throwing the seed to the left with the left hand and to the right with the right hand in a very rhythmic and seemingly efficient manner.

Having had the notion of being a doctor or a vet firmly knocked out of my head, because I enjoyed working on the farm I wondered if I could be a farmer. My parents pointed out that to own your own farm takes a lot of money, which we didn't have, and farm labourers earned very poor wages. Their advice was to avoid this. There was no reference to their own ancestors having worked in agriculture but my mother at least must have known about her own grandmother's background. Perhaps she was still ashamed to say that her mother was the illegitimate daughter of a dairymaid.

Bored

The time I hated most was Saturday afternoons when I always became incredibly bored. The reason was that some of my pals would go off to the football with their dads and some went to the matinee in the cinema. Saturday was my dad's busiest day delivering a double supply of bread to the shops and he didn't get home till late afternoon. I wasn't allowed to go to the cinema since my parents were in the Christian Brethren and the cinema was 'worldly', as was football and just about anything else you might enjoy. I often spent Saturday afternoons watching my mother cooking and baking and I think I developed an interest in cooking from then.

After the matinee and football were over we all gathered outside our door, which was under the upstairs landing. Tommy O'Neill, who lived at the front of the building, would recall the thrilling film he had been watching that afternoon. He was a great storyteller and held us spellbound for long periods of time. My father sometimes came home from work then and had to step over us to get into the house. He listened for a minute or two, and then said to Tommy, 'You'd make a great gospel preacher, sir.'

Neighbours

Most of our neighbours were decent hard-working people but one close neighbour had a bit of a problem with alcohol and became aggressive after drinking. He wore a thick leather belt and frequently removed it to give his children a beating, especially his son. This was extremely upsetting for us as children to hear. On one occasion he was playing his radio loudly and the boy was getting a leathering so my father, who was in bed trying to get to sleep, knocked on the wall. There was a sudden crashing sound against our wall and then silence, to our great relief. We later learned that he was infuriated by my father knocking and threw the radio at the wall, smashing it. As his fury was then levelled at us he stopped beating his son.

On one occasion a neighbour acquired a horse and cart. I have no idea where it, or the money to buy it, came from, but he planned to start a business selling things from the cart. He had no idea how to look after a horse but had obviously seen films of horses being broken in, so in Wild West style he had the horse running round in circles on the communal back green at the end of a rope, holding a whip in his other hand. Needless to say it served no purpose since the horse was already broken in. The poor animal was housed in a small corrugated metal shed at the far end of the green, right next to the railway line. It was a fairly quiet branch line but every time a train passed the horse was terrified. Fortunately for the horse, our neighbour was no businessman and it was soon sold to buy more alcohol.

There were several pubs in the neighbourhood and, as with many working-class areas, most of the drinking was on Friday and Saturday nights and sometimes there were fights when the men came out of the pubs. I know my mother was always keen to get us home 'before the pubs came out'. For years, I thought that they were locked in the pub and weren't allowed out till closing time.

On the whole the neighbours got on fairly well and any tensions were usually triggered by disputes between children. One Saturday evening two boys were fighting and the mothers came out to intervene, with each mother taking the side of her son. They started shouting and threatening each other, saying the husband would sort them out. Shortly after this the two husbands came home from the pub the best of friends, supporting each other as they staggered up the road. On hearing their wives' versions of events they came outside and one challenged the other to a fight. This challenge was accepted but they were too drunk to fight so agreed to postpone to the Sunday morning.

On Sunday morning at ten o'clock they duly appeared, shirtsleeves rolled up ready for the fight. The neighbours including the children all gathered around as they took up their positions and started throwing punches, but with only an occasional blow. It was quite a frightening experience for me to see two grown men fighting but I still wanted to be there and watch. One of the wives fainted and the fight came to an end with no real winner, but with honour satisfied. Meanwhile the two boys who started the whole thing were playing together at the other end of the green ignoring the commotion they were responsible for.

More Medical Matters

One of our friends, Barbara, a girl in my class at primary school, lived in one of the smart council houses across the road. She usually played with the girls or in joint games with the boys. One day she said she hadn't been feeling well and was very thirsty. She had to keep running home to go to the toilet and for a drink of water. Her mother noticed this and was also aware that Barbara had lost some weight, so took her to the doctor. As they walked into the consulting room she rushed past the doctor to the sink saying, 'I must have a drink of water or I'll die.'

The doctor said, 'This little girl's suffering from hysteria.' He examined her but found nothing wrong and gave her mother advice on managing Barbara's 'hysteria'.

Later that evening she became increasingly drowsy and could not be roused.

The first we knew of the unfolding drama was when we heard the clang, clang of the ambulance bell as it came racing up the road. It came to a screeching halt outside their house and we watched anxiously as we saw someone being carried out on a stretcher. Poor Barbara was in a diabetic coma but fortunately she got to hospital in the nick of time and her life was saved with minutes to spare. She came out of hospital two or three weeks later and from then on had to be given regular injections of insulin and stick to a very strict diet with all her food being weighed.

My mother was always willing to help anyone with a need, or just in need of a friend, and she befriended one of our primary school teachers, Miss Simpson. She got to know her when I was in her class but the friendship continued after I moved on. Like most teachers at the time she was unmarried and lived alone. I was some-times sent to her house with a cake or some home cooking. Miss Simpson started having bouts of illness when she had abdominal pain and felt very sick. They would last for some time and then settle for a while and the doctor could find nothing wrong with her, putting it down to 'nerves'.

The regular GP sometimes took on a trainee assis-tant whom my mother always referred to as 'the wee helper.' One such wee helper had impressed Mum and she persuaded Miss Simpson to go to him for a second opinion. This she did and he said, 'I think I know what's wrong with you, you may have gallstones. I'll refer you to a specialist.' She saw the surgeon in due course and after an X-ray confirmed the diagnosis she had surgery to remove her gallbladder and all was well.

My mother loved a good old chinwag and I often heard these and other medical tales. She usually got her medical facts and terminology wrong. One misunderstanding was regarding her ulcer. She was sure there was a difference of opinion between two doctors because one said she had a duodenal ulcer and another said she had a peptic ulcer. They usually mean the same thing. A second misunderstanding concerned a man who visited from time to time. He was epileptic and she said he took 'efiletic' fits. Homoeopathy was another word that caused her problems and she referred to it as 'homothapy'. One of her brothers, Wee Jimmy, had died at around twelve years old of meningitis and when she spoke of him she always said, 'He died of manygitis.'

Her concern for other people's problems, medical and otherwise, obviously rubbed off on me and my desire to be a doctor resurfaced from time to time. But I was always discouraged.

Another Cousin

Mum's brother Uncle Tam was a favourite with us. For most of our time at primary school he was unmarried and lived about 400 yards up the road. He was a miner and very generous, giving us regular pocket money and good presents at birthdays and Christmas.

He appeared one day when I was about ten, and informed Mum that he was getting married. He would have been in his mid forties at this time. She looked pleased and asked him who the lucky lady was. He said, 'Agnes Arbuckle.'

Mum looked disappointed for a few seconds but quickly regained her composure and said, 'That's nice, Tam. When did you meet her again?'

He replied, 'I met her in the Post Office two months ago and she told me her husband had died.'

The background to this was that in his twenties he had been going out with a girl called Agnes for a couple of years and they were engaged to be married. Suddenly, and shortly before the date of the wedding, she broke off the engagement and married a much older man, a local butcher, Mr Arbuckle. The new Mr and Mrs Arbuckle had a baby nine months after the marriage and Mum said, 'People were convinced the new husband was too old and the baby was Uncle Tam's. When the pram was left outside shops they would pull back the covers to have a look. But there was no mistaking the baby, he was definitely an Arbuckle.'

Now that the elderly husband had died Uncle Tam and Agnes started their relationship again. The son, Andrew, who had been the object of earlier curiosity, was now in his late teens and Mum invited them for tea in the single end. The adult conversation was boring to me but Andrew was good fun. I had a searchlight truck and toy aeroplanes and he set up a string across the room from the pulley near ceiling level to the cold water tap and had the aeroplane gliding down the string while we tried to catch it in the beam of the searchlight. Having an older cousin like this was great fun.

A year after Tam and Agnes were married, Andrew came to live with us for a short time. I wasn't told why but I often went with him to the nearest telephone kiosk. At first I didn't understand, but then he told me his mum was having a baby. Sadly she lost the baby and her age was against her having another.

Whenever our families met up Andrew, although considerably older, was always willing to amuse us and this continued even when he went off to do his National Service. He would sit and tell us about the train journey home saying, 'The train went very fast, doing sixty miles per hour. That's one mile every minute,' then he went out with us and got all our pals lined up making a train and we choo-choo'd up and down the street.

At a later date after we had moved away from High Blantyre I composed my poem, *My Childhood Games* which is on my website:

www.ascottishdoctor.com/primary-school-days

Chapter 4
Holidays

Wanlockhead

Summer holidays were always to the picturesque, former lead-mining village of Wanlockhead next to Leadhills. Wanlockhead is the highest village in Scotland at 1,531

Image 4-1: Wanlockhead approaching from Mennock Pass

feet above sea level and boasted the highest inhabited house in Scotland. My mother's parents were from there and her sister, Aunt Jean, still lived there at 3 Fraser Terrace, so for a few weeks every summer we went 'up' to Wanlockhead. It lies about forty miles south of Blantyre but being the highest village is obviously higher in altitude.

I tend to look back on Wanlockhead as a place of great freedom where we could roam the hills with safety, and we certainly enjoyed our holidays there, but it also had many potential dangers. Parts of the village were potted with old mine ventilation shafts, protected by inadequate rickety wooden fences, and there were three dams, two of which were covered by pond weed, and would have been lethal for a child falling in. The other dam for trout fishing was very deep with steep sides and a narrow path along the edge.

One day we were out for a walk. Mum and Aunt Jean with Isabel, John and I were walking along the narrow path by the fishing dam with one of the reeded dams just a little ahead. John suddenly ran off in that direction. On reaching that dam he walked straight towards it. I had a feeling of panic and could hear the panic in Mum's voice too as we called to him to stop. He didn't see any danger and kept walking right in among the reeds and then he was in the dam! My panic took over as I saw my little brother sinking. We all ran, Isabel and I arriving first, by which time the water was up to his waist. Fortunately because he was near the edge we were able to grab his hands and pull him out. There was a great feeling of relief all round and John, who had a real fright, learned a valuable lesson.

Picnics

The highlights of the holidays were the picnics to Mennock Pass, especially walking to the Mossy Burn which is about half a mile outside the village. Climbing the hills was also great fun especially when we reached the top and looked down into the valley on the other side. On

Image 4-2: Mennock Water and Mennock Pass

special occasions and when there was no chance of rain, a taxi was hired and we were taken right down into Mennock Pass for our picnic. When we were young children we were taken by my mother and Aunt Jean and her husband, Uncle Tom. We called him Uncle Tom to distinguish him from my mother's brother, Uncle Tam. Both were actually Thomas, but shortened to Tom (polite) or Tam (local dialect).

My father rarely went with us on these picnics. I can only recall two occasions and that was after pressure from my mother. I have always treasured those memories of him playing with us at the burn, making a separate channel for us to sail our little home-made wooden boats.

He considered this sort of activity a frivolous waste of time and spent most of his one week per year holiday preaching. Walking was a favourite pastime of his and some days he walked the three miles to the neighbouring village of Leadhills to preach. Other days were spent preaching in Wanlockhead. The highlight of his holiday was walking through Mennock Pass to Sanquhar and preaching in the streets there. This was a walk of about nine miles each way. He also went a little further afield to other villages. Many times he was caught in the rain on his way back, though occasionally he took the bus or was offered a lift by a passing motorist.

The Brethren Church was Ebenezer Hall in Leadhills, and on Sundays he went there morning and evening, walking both ways each time. He usually went on his own in the morning to the Communion service but the whole family went in the evening and we walked along the disused railway line through a cutting with rock sides rising vertically on either side.

Sometimes as a special treat Mum and Aunt Jean took us to Sanquhar for the day. There were shops there and it was a good place to spend some of our holiday money. We also visited a cousin of Uncle Tom's who was caretaker of the Sanquhar Memorial Institute. This was exciting because while the adults were having a right good chinwag Isabel, John and I explored the large building which contained various rooms for games including billiards, darts and carpet bowls. The last bus back was often packed and the old engine struggled to get the vehicle up some of the hills of Mennock Pass. There were occasions when the male passengers had to get off and help push the bus up the steep hill at the north end of the pass.

Freedom

When we were a bit older we enjoyed roaming the village and surrounding hills on our own. In August just before we had to return to Blantyre to go back to school, the shooting season began and the Duke of Buccleugh's shooting parties would arrive for the grouse shooting. Being older I was allowed to go beating with other boys from the village. The shooters, usually known as *guns* each took up their position behind a *butt*, which was a screen built with peat blocks. When given the signal we would run through the heather sending the grouse into the air to get shot. We shouted, clapped our hands, waved flags and beat the ground with sticks making as much noise as possible. It was exhilarating as we watched the grouse rise into the air, but not so joyful watching them fall to the ground, wings still flapping. We earned a little pocket money for this.

When I was around twelve or thirteen I went out with the Wanlockhead Co-op delivery van some days and helped by taking the orders to the houses. It was a horse-drawn van and the delivery man Mr Armstrong was very kind and let me take the reins when going from one street to the next. I'm not sure that my actions actually had any effect because, as is usually the case with horses doing a regular run, it knew the route and understood exactly where to go and when to stop, but I enjoyed the experience. It reminded me of Dick the farm horse doing the milk round in Blantyre. He knew exactly where to stop.

At the end of the run the van was taken to the old smithy and garaged there. This was the smithy visited by

Image 4-3: Former smithy. Now the Visitor Centre and Museum of Lead Mining. School in the background.

Robert Burns in the winter of 1888−89 in his capacity as exciseman. He composed a poem to persuade the farrier to turn his horse's shoes to give them a better grip on the frozen surface. The poem and background to it are on my website: www.ascottishdoctor.com/holidays. The smithy is now the Wanlockhead Visitor Centre and Museum of Lead Mining.

The horse was taken up the road to the stable, which was behind the bowling green and former curling rink. Mr Armstrong usually got up on the horse at the smithy and rode him back to his stable, but on the days I was out with him he helped me up and I rode the horse, but only with him leading, or sometimes he sat up on the horse behind me. The first time he put me up I was nervous because it seemed so high and I didn't have a good head for heights, but I got used to it and quickly came to enjoy my horse rides.

Sanitation

The village of Wanlockhead, for most of my childhood, had no electricity, no gas, no inside water supply and very few flushing toilets. There was a sink in the kitchen, not connected to the drainage system, and water had to be brought into the house in buckets from an outside tap shared by two families. There was a second bucket under the hole in the sink to catch the waste water.

The toilet was an outhouse next to, and the same size as, the coal cellar. It consisted of a bucket under a board with a bottom-sized hole in it. In later years when I was eighteen I took my girlfriend on holiday for the first time and she needed to go to the toilet late in the evening when it was dark. She was given a small torch and pointed in the right direction, only to find herself stumbling into the coal cellar and on to a pile of coal.

When the bucket had filled to a certain level it had to be emptied. One method was having a 'burial' when a hole would be dug in the garden and the contents emptied into it. Wanlockhead gardens produced the best vegetables in the south of Scotland! The second, more common method was by going to the burn at night. There were two significant burns. The Mossy Burn rises above a fishing dam and runs down through Mennock Pass as Mennock Water. It had crystal-clear water and was always pure and clean. The other burn, Wanlock Water, runs down the valley through the village and past the lead mines. This was the burn used by many in the village for emptying their buckets. We always referred to this as the 'dirty' burn and never played anywhere near this one. Much later, in the 1950s and 1960s, the practice ceased when homes started to get septic tanks and inside flush toilets.

When visiting Wanlockhead recently I was impressed by the contrast between the 1940s and now.

Wanlock Water Then and Now
Down through the village flowed old Wanlock Water,
Not a place to linger or stay to potter.
Dry toilets then, in a closet outside,
With a bucket and board to sit astride
Were used by many in old Wanlockhead,
Making a task they considered with dread.

It had to be done but how, when and where?
The burn was the place if done with some care.
Making their way in the darkness at night,
Taking their buckets but well out of sight,

They emptied them there again and again,
In soiled Wanlock Burn that flowed down the glen.

Years have gone by and I now stand beside
A pure crystal stream I view with great pride.
Museum of Lead Mining stands nearby,
With visitors learning of days gone by.
Walking beside a disused railway line
They follow the burn to see an old mine.

Adults sit on the grass in pleasant weather,
Admiring the hills and the purple heather.
Children play on the grass along the banks.
People panning for gold hope to give thanks
For the treasure they find, just now and then,
In clean Wanlock Burn that flows down the glen.

James Graham 2012

Electricity

Aunt Jean had a radio and this was a real treat since we weren't allowed one at home. It was powered by an accumulator, a wet lead battery like a car battery. A van came up from Sanquhar once a week and took them away to recharge, leaving a fully charged one that had to last a week. Because of this the old valve type of radio, before the days of transistors, was only used for short periods each day. I think there were a few daytime programmes like *Housewife's Choice* and *Music While You Work* that could be played while my father was out.

103

On some evenings there was an evangelistic programme on Radio Luxemburg which often featured Billy Graham, long before his big crusades. My parents, even my father, enjoyed that but we children preferred the music.

Because there was no electricity and therefore no street lights, when it was overcast it was very dark but on a clear night the moon and the stars were magnificent. With the building of a radar station on Green Lowther Hill, electricity was eventually brought into the village in the late 1950s.

It was during these dark evenings that we sat round the fire or beneath the paraffin lamp listening to tales of times gone by; tales of our ancestors, of Burke and Hare, and of the Covenanters.

Sheep and Lambs

The stillness was almost palpable at night and during lambing and shortly after, the only sound to be heard was the bleating of lambs looking for their mothers. As a young child I was often upset at the thought of those poor lambs lost on the hills without their mothers, but when it went silent I would be told that everything was fine, they had found each other.

The locals used the sheep, among other things, to predict the weather. If they were high on the hills the weather would remain good or take a turn for the better, but if they were down in the valley the weather would be bad. They often grazed just outside the house and I remember once trying to *clap* or pat a cuddly-looking little lamb only to have the furious mother charge me. I was surprised because I didn't realise the mother had no way of knowing I wasn't trying to harm her offspring. Fortunately I managed to get into the house just in time. Aunt Jean had a favourite sheep called Bunty which she fed, but Bunty soon became a nuisance and frequently followed her into the house.

A Family Day Out

Dad's Uncle Willie had always been kind to us at Christmas and birthdays but I had never seen him. While we were on holiday one year when I was about eleven we had one of those rare events when all five of us went out for a day as a family. The only other time this happened was when travelling to or from Wanlockhead for our holidays.

Uncle Willie, who wrote regularly to Dad, suggested we visit him while at Wanlockhead, since it was much nearer to Langholm than Blantyre. He had never married and was in the early stages of Parkinson's disease and putting his affairs in order. There was a legal document he would like Dad to sign. It was probably his will but as children we weren't told. Dad agreed and hired a car to take us all to Langholm to visit him. Uncle Willie was delighted to see us and gave us presents, and then we were allowed to go outside to play while the adults attended to the business in hand. All this adult talk was boring!

Much more interesting was the car journey as we passed places we had never seen or heard of before; places with strange names like made-up names from a story book. They included: Locharbriggs, Lockerbie, Ecclefechan and the Devil's Beef Tub. This last one was interesting because when our parents explained things about it we were reminded of some of the stories we'd heard in Wanlockhead about our ancestors and the Lowther Hills.

This deep hollow formed by four hills gets its name from the Border Reivers. The Johnstone clan who were referred to as 'devils' by their enemies used this deep hollow to hide stolen cattle, hence the name Devil's Beef Tub. It is also associated with the Covenanters and in 1685 a Covenanter, John Hunter was fleeing from the pursuing soldiers and tried to climb the steep side to escape but was shot dead. There is a monument to him on the rim of the Beef Tub. The Scottish novelist Walter Scott, in one of his novels, describes an incident following the failed 1745 Jacobite rebellion. A Jacobite soldier rolled all the way down the steep hillside amid a hail of enemy gunfire and escaped alive but injured. The Beef Tub is sometimes called 'MacCleran's Loup' for this reason.

Grandpa Watson

I wrote one of my first poems in Wanlockhead when I was about eleven. We had been taught the basics of poetry in primary school and I obviously felt ready to give it a go. My grandfather had become too old and frail to stay in his home in High Blantyre, so went to live out his final years with Aunt Jean in Wanlockhead, the place where he was born and where he'd started work as a lead miner. It seemed to rain a lot in Wanlockhead and one day my younger brother John and I were being too noisy, annoying our grandfather who shouted at me. John on the other hand could do no wrong and this upset me so my mother said, 'Why don't you go to the room and write a poem?' So I did:

Favouritism
Johnny Watson is my grandpa's name,
His favourite is wee Johnny Graham.
You see, our Johnny is called after him,
And that's the reason for the fav'ritism.

Grandpa had gangrene in his feet and was in severe pain. The doctor visited regularly and dressed the gangrenous feet. He also gave him a painkilling liquid which I assume was laudanum (tincture of opium). The doctor lived in the neighbouring village of Leadhills. One very dark night Grandpa was in extreme pain and his supply of laudanum was quickly used up. Uncle Tom went out to a public telephone to call the doctor, and came back to say the doctor would give him more but someone had to go and get it. I went with my father and we walked the six-mile round trip in pitch dark to get more opium. So much for the old-school family doctors who went out all hours of the day and night!

If I was the doctor, I would go and see the patient and take the medication to him, I thought.

The new radar station at Lowther Hill was being built at this time and Uncle Tom was keen to see the progress. Although he was only forty-six he had angina and was no longer fit enough to climb the hill. A niece from his side of the family was visiting, and she booked the local car hire man to drive him up the construction track to see it on 22 July 1948. He thoroughly enjoyed the experience but as he walked back into the house he looked pale and clammy. Within seconds of sitting in his usual chair he slumped forward, dead, in front of us all. This was my first experience of a cardiac arrest. It was a frightening experience especially since the adults were in a state of panic.

Grandpa's health deteriorated rapidly and he too died, just a few weeks later on 9 August 1948 at eighty-five years of age. It was fitting that he died in Wanlockhead, his place of birth, but he was taken back to High Blantyre to be buried beside his wife and two deceased children.

Amusements

Being in Scotland and among the hills it rained quite often at Wanlockhead so we had to find ways of amusing ourselves indoors. One place was the wash house where Uncle Tom kept a variety of tools and I would try to make things such as a kite or small wooden boat to sail when we went to the Mossy Burn. Aunt Jean also sold cigarettes and Barr's soft drinks from her home and the drinks were kept in the wash house; very tempting.

Another interesting place was the loft. The house consisted of a living room with two hole-in-the-wall beds, a bedroom and a kitchen. Access to the loft was by means of a ladder from the kitchen. The loft was partly floored and had a bed and chest of drawers as well as odds and ends stored in it.

It was exciting exploring the loft, and one item of special interest was an old wind-up gramophone and some records. One set of records in particular amused us a lot. They were comedies about a man called Casey. The funniest was one entitled *Casey Goes to the Dentist*. He had toothache and went looking for a dentist. When he found one there was a notice saying, 'Teeth extracted without pain' which he took to mean without pay-ing. The comedy centred around the play on *pain* and *paying*. There were also some Harry Lauder records and a variety of card and board games.

We played board games, bagatelle and quoits. The quoits board hung next to a print of *The Monarch of the Glen* and Uncle Tom always said, 'The first person to ring the deer's antlers wins the game.' I was always fidgety and if I was getting a bit bored would sit and rattle the handles of the chest of drawers or rock on the front legs of the chair. This frequently led to a telling-off and I did fall under the bed sometimes if the chair slipped from under me.

In my later teens when we had stopped going to Wanlockhead for family holidays, I reminisced on them and wrote a poem, *Wanlockhead Holidays*. It is rather too long for this book but can be found on my website: www.ascottishdoctor.com/holidays

Other Annual Events

Apart from the summer holiday which was the biggest annual event there were other highlights. The next event after the summer was Hallowe'en. We dressed in old adult clothes and wore masks which we made ourselves to go *guising*, or what we called 'going out for our Hallowe'en'. After waiting for darkness we went round the doors asking for our Hallowe'en. Sometimes we were given something at the door, usually a piece of fruit, nuts or money—sixpence or threepence—but more often we were invited in and asked to do something such as singing, telling jokes or reciting a poem. I was rubbish at singing so usually recited a poem. Our lanterns were, more often than not, jam jars with a candle in them and string round the rim. When we were a little older and helped out at the farm we were allowed to take what in Scotland is called a turnip but in most other places a swede. Taking out the centre of a turnip and making a face was hard work. Having recently carved out a pumpkin for my granddaughter, this was child's play compared to those turnips.

Next was Guy Fawkes Night on 5 November. We didn't have money for a lot of fireworks but we made a guy and gathered firewood to have a bonfire, usually in the middle of the communal green or in the field behind the coal cellars. Fireworks consisted of a few bangers, some sparklers and perhaps if enough families clubbed together we could have two or three rockets.

The big event for us as children was Christmas, of course. As with all children excitement mounted over the weeks before, and one of our big hobbies as small children was cutting out Santas from newspapers or magazines. On Christmas Eve we hung up our stockings by the fireplace and a pillowslip near our beds. We were fortunate because, although my parents didn't have much money, we had several aunts and uncles. Some had no children, or their children had grown up, so we received quite a few presents. Christmas was not a holiday in Scotland at that time so Santa usually came shortly before my father left for work at 4 am.

New Year's Day was the public holiday in Scotland and festivities began on New Year's Eve, or Hogmanay. Most families stayed at home till *the bells*, church bells were rung at midnight to usher in the New Year, and then they'd go out first-footing, visiting friends and neighbours and taking a bottle with them.

Within our Evangelical Christian community we had a Watchnight service which started at 11 pm and went on till about half past midnight. This was a Christian concert with singing, poetry, or people telling of their experiences during the past year. There was a prayer thanking God for the blessings of the past year and asking His blessing and guidance for the year to come. Then we had tea with sandwiches or a sausage roll and cakes. Afterwards we went home or visited friends taking non-alcoholic ginger wine.

Aunt Jean usually came to stay with us over New Year but she, Mum and Aunt Jenny didn't go to the Watchnight service. They preferred to stay at home to bring in the New Year quietly and have a *wee greet* (cry), thinking of loved ones who had died.

The next highlight of the year was the Easter holiday. Nothing much happened at Easter but it was a very welcome break from school.

Chapter 5

Secondary School Days

Calder Street Junior Secondary School

Decision Time

At age eleven a decision had to be made about secondary education. Any idea of going on to higher education, and especially any idea of becoming a doctor, had been quashed in my earlier years. To my parents, giving their sons a chance in life was to encourage them to learn a trade. The saying was, 'If you learn a trade you can leave and come back to it if other things don't work out, but if you have no trade you've nothing to fall back on.' My father had been a building labourer before becoming a bread delivery man and my mother a servant in a big house at Blantyre.

The options for secondary education were one of the two senior secondary schools in Hamilton, St John's Grammar School and Hamilton Academy, three miles away, or the local Calder Street Junior Secondary School. Forms were sent out to parents to complete indicating their preference. We didn't have the eleven-plus examination taken by pupils in England and Wales but those who opted for the senior secondary schools had a qualifying examination to sit.

My mother said to me, 'You don't want to go to the Academy, son, do you?'

I replied, 'No', because I'd been taught that people like us do manual work, and that was it: settled. Indeed my parents appeared to have the opinion that working-class children didn't have the *brains* of children from more affluent backgrounds.

I had a friend at secondary school who lived in a bigger, privately owned house, and we went together to the school dance in our final year. My mother said, 'Oh well, son, he may be brainier than you but you're certainly better looking than him.' The fact was, my results were consistently better than his, but my mother assumed that because he was from a more affluent home he must be more intelligent. Although my parents didn't vote they read the *Daily Express,* and appeared to have a preference for a Conservative government over Socialist. My mother's comment was, 'The Tories have the brains.'

Those of us who opted for junior secondary school still had an examination to sit because pupils in Calder Street were streamed A, B or C group according to ability, with A being the highest. I was in the A group and we did English, maths, general science, history, geography, French, religious education (RE), music, woodwork for boys and domestic science for girls, technical drawing, art and physical education. When I reflect on those days I am amazed at, and proud of, the breadth of education we received at our junior secondary school.

I recently read the memoirs of a Glasgow man who came from a working-class background. He passed the qualifying examination and went to a senior secondary school in Glasgow. After successfully completing his secondary and higher education he became a Baptist minister, but later went into teaching and became a headmaster. He talked about the pressure from teachers and parents to work hard and pass the qualifying examination. When commenting on the later introduction of comprehensive schools, he wasn't very keen on them but said, *'The comprehensive school would have an important role in social engineering, eliminating the damaging social stigma associated with screening children into the Junior Secondary schools.'* [5] It made me bristle.

Clearly, going to junior secondary school was a dead end, in the sense that there was no direct way from there into higher education or of getting any formal educational qualifications, but I was never aware of any stigma. My friends and I went there because that was our choice or that of our parents, not because we failed to qualify for senior secondary. Indeed I am convinced that almost all of us who were in the A group would have passed the qualifying examination for senior secondary if we or our parents had chosen that route.

---

[5] *Comfy Glasgow . . . Gaun Elsewhere* , George Mitchell, Comfy George Publishing Co.

In Image 5-1 below, I am the last boy on the right in the back row, and the teacher on the left is Mr Wattie

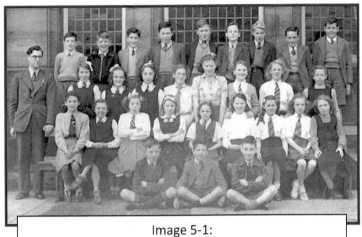

Image 5-1:
Class 1A Calder Street Junior Secondary School 1950

('Wee Wattie') who taught us maths and RE. He was a good if strict teacher but I got off to an unfortunate start with him. RE then was entirely about the Christian faith and especially the Bible. In his class he started at Genesis and taught us that the stories in these early chapters were myths, which was what was taught at most universities and theological seminaries. However this was seen as an attack on the inspiration and authority of the Bible by conservative evangelicals such as Brethren, Baptists, Pentecostals and evangelicals in the Church of Scotland.

Those parents were very annoyed and had discussions which led to my father being delegated to go to the school and protest. Following his meeting with the headmaster, Mr Moffat (another Big Tam), Mr Wattie was obviously spoken to because I was called out in front of the class and he said, 'It seems I've been teaching things which are wrong. Please let me know if I teach anything wrong in the future.' I'm sure there was a large element of sarcasm in that but it is just possible he was trying to avoid further confrontation with a group of parents who had very strong conservative religious views. The whole incident certainly embarrassed me but to his credit it was never mentioned again and he didn't treat me any differently.

I did well in all subjects but better in those that required me to grasp concepts or involving memory, such as maths, science, French and English language. I found subjects requiring a lot of reading such as history and English literature a bit more challenging. This was because, I discovered, I was quite a *slow reader*.

Physical Education (PE)

Looking back at the PE we had at secondary school I get annoyed. In primary school, PE was enjoyable because it was simple physical jerks but in secondary school it was almost entirely gymnastics and I hated it. I would have been happy to do double maths instead because I was overweight and clumsy. I think this put me off all forms of sport until I discovered cycling when I was fifteen, but more of that later. On the few occasions we were taken outside for athletics I enjoyed that, especially hurdles, because I had long legs; not that I ever won any races but at least I could do it. I became very competitive in races and did my utmost to be *second last*.

During these years I had some pubertal breast development which was compounded by my being overweight so I developed a pair of *boobs*, or *moobs* as they are called today. In PE the boys only wore shorts so this was obvious to everyone and I encountered a bit of ribbing about it. Most of the time I didn't find this offensive or intimidating and I joined in the jokes because they were made by my close friends.

At one point other boys who were not in my circle of friends joined in and then I felt the joking had gone too far and told them so. However I can see that the line between good fun and bullying can be very fine and if the jokes had been nasty or were meant to be hurtful I'm sure I would have been refusing to go to school on PE days. I know this is a situation many boys find themselves in and it's something schools and parents need to be aware of.

St Patrick's Day

When we lived in High Blantyre the walk to Calder Street Junior Secondary School in Low Blantyre was a bit too far to come home at lunchtime so I had school lunch. After we moved to Cowan Wilson Avenue, nearer the school, there was time to get home for lunch and a group of us did so. We had to make sure we left home to get back to school on time because the teachers were strict and we would get the belt if we were late without good reason. There was one day per year, however, when we could get away with being late returning and that was 17 March; St Patrick's Day.

The politics and religious tensions of Northern Ireland had considerable influence on the west of Scotland. Roman Catholics and Protestants regarded the other as the enemy, but for the most part we played together when away from school or we ignored each other. However on St Patrick's Day tensions tended to be heightened and it was common to be asked if you were a Mick or a Dan, and giving the wrong answer sometimes resulted in fights.

We had to walk past St Joseph's Roman Catholic School to get to our school and on every other day we crossed each other's paths without incident but to avoid confrontations on St Patrick's Day we tended to return late, either to time it so they were back in class or because we took a detour to avoid them. When the teacher asked why we were late we said we'd been confronted by Catholic boys and had to take a long way back to avoid a fight. That explanation was accepted on that day only.

Corporal Punishment

Nowadays, maintaining discipline in class is no longer straightforward, partly because the threat of corporal punishment has been removed and partly because of a changing society and its approach to authority. As a result, some teachers find their work in the classroom is challenging, and indeed are sometimes afraid of their pupils, both because of the threat of violence and the threat of litigation in response to any physical contact. I have a lot of sympathy for the teachers who can have a difficult time especially in some secondary schools.

During my school days between 1943 and 1953 discipline was maintained with the belt, or at least the credible threat of it. This was a thick leather strap about two inches wide and about two feet long and was used in both primary and secondary schools. There were different levels of severity of the punishment depending on the type of misconduct and the propensity of the teacher to hand out physical punishment. Common misdemeanours were talking in class, not paying attention, reading comics under the desk, not doing homework, not bringing the correct books, annoying other pupils and worst of all being cheeky to the teacher.

The simplest was a single stroke of the belt on the palm of one hand. This allowed the hand to drop under the impact making it less painful. If more severe punishment was required it was given to crossed hands. One hand was placed under the hand receiving the punishment to prevent it falling away, making the impact stronger. The next step up would be two or possibly three strokes.

The belt was rarely used in the lower levels of primary school but had occasional use in the upper two years (Primary 6 & 7), although in our school, High Blantyre Primary School, the teacher of Primary 7, Mr Ferrier, never used the belt because he had his artificial arm instead.

On the whole the system worked well in my two schools and I was unaware of any abuse of the belt by teachers. There was one occasion however, when Mr Robertson, our technical teacher, overstepped the mark. We had never known him to use the belt before this, since he could maintain discipline simply by the tone of his voice. However this worked because the thick leather strap was always visible hanging on the side of his desk and we had the expectation that the next step would be the belt.

On this occasion he was explaining a concept and with a slip of the tongue said something which we found funny. Most of us simply smiled but William Evans who was always well behaved suddenly guffawed loudly. Mr Robertson lost his temper and called William out to get the belt. He gave him four or five very hard strokes on crossed hands, so severe they caused bruising. William, as well as many of the girls in class, was crying. Needless to say, his parents took up the matter with the headmaster and Mr Robertson was disciplined.

This was the only instance I'm aware of a teacher crossing the line but there were reports of teachers abusing their position in other schools. Later in life after my marriage my wife Mary talked of one boy in her class who came from a very poor home and was always dirty and badly dressed. The teacher took a strong dislike to him and beat him daily, upsetting the other children. Sadly his parents didn't seem to care and never made any effort to remedy the situation.

My thoughts on corporal punishment are that for the vast majority it did no harm and gave us a respect for our teachers and adults in general. We learned that there were boundaries that must not be crossed. However there is no doubt that more care was needed to control bullying and abusive teachers who were of course in a minority, but did serious and lasting harm to the children they abused.

The Scotts

After the death of my maternal grandfather, Mum's sister Aunt Jenny and her husband Uncle George took over his house in Broompark Road, High Blantyre, which had lain empty from the time he went to live with Aunt Jean in Wanlockhead. They converted it into a grocery shop. Uncle George was a short-tempered, rather impatient man and one year he fell out with his tomato supplier. He decided to get his own tomatoes for the shop by taking a bus to Lesmahagow on his Wednesday half-day off, to purchase them directly from the grower. This was a round trip of thirty-five miles.

The problem was he could only carry two baskets and he needed four so I was asked to go with him as we were on holiday from school. I didn't like this at all but I did get a few shillings for my trouble. Fortunately it only lasted a few weeks because he realised he had bitten off his nose to spite his face, and this method was not cost-effective. He apologised to the supplier and normal deliveries were resumed.

Because they had to keep the shop open all the time, Aunt Jenny and Uncle George took their holidays at different times and Uncle George came to us for lunch while Aunt Jenny was away. One day while I was playing at the farm I was walking round the perimeter wall of the dung midden and fell in feet first, right up above my knees. I was wearing Wellingtons and they filled with manure and I was stuck. There was no one else around and since it was well away from the farmhouse my calls for help couldn't be heard. After struggling for ages I managed to pull on the wall and drag myself out, leaving my Wellingtons behind. Lying on the wall I plunged my arms into the smelly stuff and retrieved them. Realising the state I was in I went to an outside tap and tried to wash my arms, legs, Wellingtons and socks at the farm, but was still honking when I arrived back home. Uncle George had almost finished eating but couldn't stand the smell so got up and stormed out, slamming the door.

On another occasion we had a joiner in repairing one of the set-in beds and he was doing some hammering. Again Uncle George stormed out saying he would not tolerate such noise. My mother apologised to the joiner pointing out very quickly, 'He's no' ma man, he's ma sister's man.'

A Council House

The old tenement buildings were showing their age and they gradually became unfit for human habitation. Damp was a serious problem and I recall the wallpaper coming off the wall despite my parents' best efforts to keep it on with paste and even tacks. It was while I was at Calder Street School, when I was thirteen, that our Broompark Road building in High Blantyre was condemned and we moved to a brand new council house, 13 Cowan Wilson Avenue, just behind Dr Gordon's house.

When we were in the single end in Broompark Road, life for us, like most working-class families, was difficult with little in the way of luxuries, but we were adequately fed and clothed. Even then, however, I do remember my mother having to borrow money from Uncle Tam.

On moving to the new house life became much more financially difficult for my parents. Most of the furniture in the old house had been badly infested with woodworm and had to be destroyed, so they suddenly found themselves having to furnish a living room and three bedrooms almost from scratch, not to mention bathroom and kitchen fittings, curtains and floor coverings. This couldn't be done all at once but the essentials were bought on hire purchase, which added greatly to the financial struggle.

At one point there was no money to buy me trousers for after school so I was given an old pair of dungarees and wore them with a jumper over the top part. Aunt Jenny, mum's sister, bought my brother John and me a new Sunday suit and Isabel a coat on our birthdays. The problem with this was, she was more dominant than my mother and tended to dictate which suits we should get, often in brown, which my mother disliked as did John and I. But, as they say, 'Beggars can't be choosers.' Isabel was usually happy with her coat. Being a bit older and a girl she was given more choice.

When we were in the tenement we had baths in a tin tub, filled from a kettle, in front of the fire and we were only allowed one once a week. Now we had a bathroom with a bath and hot running water we had baths much more frequently. My brother John who was nine at the time loved his baths but my mother noticed he didn't use any soap so she asked why not. He said, 'I didn't think you were supposed to use it, Oor Wullie doesn't use soap.'

John was always the entrepreneurial type and one morning when we were having our cornflakes he found a competition for a car on the packet. The idea was to place ten different features of a car in order of importance and send off the entry to Kellogg's. It looked very simple but there was only one entry per packet allowed so he reckoned that if we bought lots of packets of Kellogg's Cornflakes and sent in lots of entries we must win, so he persuaded me to chip in with my pocket money and we bought about twenty packets. Needless to say we didn't win but we did have cornflakes for breakfast, *and supper,* for a very long time.

The three bedrooms were upstairs. Mum and Dad had the largest, front room, John and I shared a smaller back room and Isabel had the smallest back room. There was no central heating and the rooms tended to be cold in winter, but a small single-bar electric fire provided some warmth. With the heavy frosts we got in winter we were able to make ice lollipops by placing egg cups full of lemonade on the bedroom window ledge.

The open coal fire in the living room had a back boiler which heated the water and this could be supplemented with an electric immersion heater. There was no gas supply. A few years after we moved into the council house, clean air regulations prevented the burning of normal coal, and smokeless fuel was very expensive so an electric fire was installed in place of the coal fire. This proved to be wholly inadequate but a few years later when our parents could afford it electric storage heaters were put in, providing better all-round heat.

DIY

I had enjoyed working with wood from primary school days and found electricity fascinating at secondary school. Following the introduction of the clean air regulations, there was no need for the coal cellar in the kitchen, so I volunteered to convert it into a walk-in cupboard. After cleaning out the coal dust I set about putting in three shelves.

As I was cutting wood the saw slipped and sliced my wrist. I was bleeding profusely and had no idea what to do so Mum gave me a towel to wrap round it and said, 'Now run round to Dr Gordon's house. He's in for his lunch.' Our house overlooked his and we could see the back of his house from upstairs at the front. Feeling rather faint, I went round the corner to his house staggering a bit as I walked.

I rang the back door bell and Mrs Gordon came to the door. As she opened the door she saw the blood seeping through the towel and said, 'You'd better come in.'

The doctor was sitting at the table enjoying a bowl of soup and said, 'What's going on here?'

'I cut my wrist and it's bleeding badly. Can you help me?'

He stood up and took me to a small consulting room which he kept for this sort of occurrence. After removing the towel he said, 'You've been very fortunate because you just missed an artery.' After cleaning it up he put three stitches in and sent me off with instructions to come to the proper surgery on Glasgow Road in a week to have the stitches removed. I thought I would like to be as knowledgeable and competent.

Not deterred I continued with my project and after completing the shelves I set about putting in lights, one light for each shelf. There was a power socket in the cupboard so, with my *vast experience* of electrical work, I put in the lights with no difficulty; or so I thought!

When I switched on the light I was surprised to find that each light bulb was dimmer than the one before. What had I done wrong?

From school science, my view of electric current was like plumbing. The positive was the water supply and the negative the drain, taking the water away. The earth was the overflow. I did then what I should have done before, read a reliable book on the subject. I had connected my lights in series but should have connected them in parallel. This corrected, the lights worked properly.

There was one further act of folly. After I put in a new light switch I didn't have a spare light bulb to check it so I put the switch in the 'off' position and stuck my finger in the lamp socket confident that I wouldn't get a shock because I had connected it properly. I didn't get a shock and, more importantly *I was still alive*. Clearly I still had a lot to learn!

Friends

Moving from the tenements in High Blantyre to a council estate in Low Blantyre caused some disruption in friendships. I lost touch with some friends but made new ones,

Image 5-2: David Livingstone Centre

mainly fellow pupils at secondary school who had gone to a different primary school but lived near us in the council estate.

Two of my farm friends John and Bill were rehoused around the same time and we kept up our friendship and visits to the farm. Two new friends were Ben Walker whom we called 'Beefy' and Jim Jackson. They didn't go to the farm but we spent time exploring our new area with the much larger River Clyde replacing the Calder. The birthplace of the famous missionary and explorer David Livingstone is beside the Clyde and it has large playing fields with swings, maypole, roundabouts, rocking horse and many other attractions. It was used by schools and Sunday schools for outings, and visitors had to pay an entry fee but we knew how to get in without paying. Further down the banks of the river were the ruins of Blantyre Priory, a fascinating place to explore. It has been said there is a tunnel under the river to Bothwell Castle and we often tried to find it but no one ever has and it's doubtful if it exists. Then there was derelict Bothwell Castle itself on the other side of the Clyde and of course the new house building site was a great attraction. We waited till the men had finished work for the day then we went exploring the partly built house. There was a watchman, of course, but he was more concerned with preventing theft, so didn't bother us.

A Dance

The school held a final year dance for the third-year pupils before we left aged fifteen. It was rather odd that my strict Brethren parents allowed me to go to this, since dancing, like the cinema, was considered worldly and not something a Christian should do. However, we had been learning Scottish country dancing in PE that year and it seemed perfectly natural to me that I should go, and I wasn't aware of any opposition from my parents.

Aunt Jenny, who was also in the Brethren, did approach my mother and say how surprised she was that she was allowing me to go. Continuing her offensive, Aunt Jenny said, 'It's a dance, you know, it isn't a party.' Now generally, well-supervised parties with children's games were allowed but never dances. Although my mother was the more submissive of the two women she could be forceful when the interests of her family were concerned so she dug her heels in and said, 'If he wants to go, he's going.'

We all enjoyed learning the dances but my sense of rhythm wasn't very good and I found some steps more difficult than others. Most of my friends considered it a useful preparation for going to dances and meeting girls in the future. The dance itself was well organised and we were all given cards with the names of film stars on to find our dance partners. This saved the embarrassment of having to approach a girl to ask her to dance. Since we were still only fourteen or fifteen most boys were still at that awkward stage around girls. I enjoyed the dance but I knew it was a one-off and that unless I rebelled against my parents, then unlike my friends I wouldn't be going to dances in the future.

Chapter 6

Bricklaying

Three Choices

Since any form of ambition to become a doctor or vet, or indeed enter any profession had been stifled, I wasn't motivated to work hard at school and my main ambition was to get to fifteen years of age and leave. I frequently questioned what I was taught, not only in the religious field but in general, and my father often said to me, 'You should be a lawyer, sir,' but this was never a serious suggestion.

On leaving school the decision had to be made as to what kind of trade I should take up. I always enjoyed working with wood and wanted to be a joiner, but during science lessons I was fascinated by electricity so thought being an electrician would be good if I couldn't be a joiner. Since we had recently moved to our new council estate, house-building was going on around us. I'd watched bricklayers at work and it looked interesting, so that was another possibility.

The school didn't offer any form of careers advice but there was a Youth Employment Service as part of the Labour Exchange. I went to see the Youth Employment

Officer armed with my three choices in order of preference; joiner, then electrician and then bricklayer. Surely I'll get something out of that, I thought, after all, they're all building trades and there's a lot of building going on.' How wrong I was!

The man was pleasant but appeared uninterested. He asked me about my hobbies and interests and then asked what kind of work I would like to do. I told him my main hobby was working with wood and he commented on how keen I appeared to be. But when I said I'd like to be an apprentice joiner he just said, 'We don't have any vacancies for that. Wouldn't you like to be a delivery boy for a grocer or butcher?'

'No,' I replied, 'but I'd also like to be an electrician.'

'I can't help you with that either. Is there anything else you'd like to do?'

'What about apprentice bricklayer?' I asked but his reply was, 'Why do you pick all the difficult ones? I can get you started as a delivery boy.' No further advice was given and I left without a job.

The problem was, I was fifteen years old and wanted to learn a trade but most employers didn't start apprentices till they were sixteen. I didn't know that and he didn't explain it to me so that I could have taken a delivery job for a year.

Apprentice Bricklayer

For the next few weeks I didn't do anything and then suddenly I had a visit from my older cousin, Walter

Scott. I didn't know him very well since he was a lot older and had already left home when I was visiting my aunt and uncle as a child. He was a foreman bricklayer with Weir Housing Corporation and said he could get me started as an apprentice bricklayer on his site in Tannochside, Uddingston. He gave me a list of the tools I would need and told me to report to the site office at 8 am the following Monday.

Getting from Blantyre to Tannochside took well over an hour and involved taking three buses. I was assigned to a squad which consisted of a gaffer or charge hand, another three bricklayers, an older apprentice and three labourers. Fortunately they were at a stage where they were about to start on the brick foundations of a new block of houses and had a bit of time to show me the basics of how to handle a trowel, mortar and bricks.

It was also fortunate that they were at this stage because seeing another squad working on scaffolding close by reminded me that I suffered from vertigo when more than a few feet off the ground. As children when we climbed trees, my pals would go right up into the upper branches but I got stuck in the lower limbs because of this. When we were playing on the building site at home my pals would go walking across the upper floor joists but I had to stay close to the wall. Now the reality of my apprenticeship hit me: I would have to go up ladders and work at heights. How would I cope?

A few days after I started the squad gaffer sent me to the office to ask for *a long staun*. The foreman, my cousin, told me to wait outside till they found one. I waited and waited till someone passed and asked me what I was waiting for. I said, 'A long staun.' He said nothing but his wry smile gave the game away and it dawned on me that *long staun* meant a long stand and that was exactly what I was getting. This was one of a series of initiation pranks usually played on new apprentices.

Bonus

The bricklaying squads were on a bonus scheme so didn't have a lot of time for teaching but once shown the basics I was put between two tradesmen to lay bricks in straight lines only, while they did the corners and vertical ends required for doors and windows. Apprentices shared in the bonus, getting a very small share in the first year and increasing each year to an equal share on completing the apprenticeship.

It was hard physical work but I enjoyed the experience and learning new skills. The squad I started with were skilled bricklayers who worked quickly and to a high standard so they earned good bonuses. The gaffer earned a higher share of the bonus than the other bricklayers and they in turn earned more than the labourers. I recall that in the April after I started the gaffer became quite excited, because his payslip showed that he had earned just over £1,000 in the previous financial year. He said, 'Wow, that's £20 a week!' That was a milestone and his highest earnings ever.

Working at Heights

Since we started on the foundations of a block of four houses I had no difficulty with heights at that stage. The first level of scaffolding was only five feet off the ground

Image 6-1: Builders' hoist

so that didn't present me with a problem and to my surprise, as we got higher I gradually adjusted to the greater elevation and the vertigo was no longer a problem.

There were few if any Health and Safety rules then and we worked from scaffolding with no guard rails.

Access was by a ladder straight up the front of the scaffolding. Bricks and mortar were sent up by means of a mechanical hoist and we often used that to go up and down at tea breaks although this was against the rules. It was a simple platform with no rails.

On one occasion when we were at roof level I was sent for wall plates which were ten-foot-long wooden planks. I stood on the platform holding the wall plates vertical and as the hoist went up I gradually lost my balance and began to sway perilously. Fortunately someone saw me and called for the hoist to be stopped and lowered. Apart from the fright, I got into terrible trouble so never tried that one again.

On the odd occasion when the hoist wasn't working the labourers had to carry the bricks and mortar in hods up the ladder to the scaffolding. Since this was much slower than the hoist the apprentices were sent to help them. Carrying a hod up a ladder was a skill which had to learned, especially stepping from the ladder on to the scaffolding.

While on the whole I did acquire a head for heights there was one job I hated. On a few occasions we didn't have any chimney pots when we'd completed the chimney and they were delivered much later when the roof was up. I was sent to put them on and this involved stepping from the ladder on to the sloping roof with a chimney pot or bucket of mortar on my shoulder. Although walking up and down the roof or along the ridge was no problem, stepping from the ladder on to the roof or from the roof back on to the ladder was always very difficult for me.

Tea Boy

One of my jobs in the first couple of years was to be tea boy for my squad. There was a *nipper* who kept the bothy clean, a hut used by workmen, and lit the fire under the hot water urn. A nipper is a child and the term probably came from the use of children for such chores in the past, but in the 1950s they were generally elderly retired men working a few hours per week. About ten minutes before tea breaks I was sent to make the tea for my lot. They each had their own cans and tea tins with varying amounts of tea and sugar so I had to learn to whom each belonged, toast cheese and heat pies and sausage rolls and so on so that everything was ready for them to start eating as soon as they came into the bothy. There was no time to waste as they'd lose money if they took too long over their break, which was usually fifteen minutes morning and afternoon and half an hour at lunchtime.

Another job apprentices were given was to run errands such as going to the shops for lemonade, pies, sausage rolls, Forfar bridies (similar to Cornish pasties) or cigarettes (Woodbine, Players, Craven A & Capstan come to mind). The men were quite generous and I was given a tip by some of them on payday which was always a Friday. At the annual holiday on Glasgow Fair week when they had their holiday money I was given a larger tip.

Epileptic Seizure

On one occasion a few weeks after I started when I was getting the tea ready for my squad, Rab, a labourer from another squad, came into the bothy slightly ahead of the others. He looked a little dazed and frightened and suddenly fell to the floor. His whole body went into a spasm, quickly followed by violent jerking movements. Fortunately the men were arriving for their tea break and one of the bricklayers, Harry, took charge immediately. He rolled Rab on his side, asked for a spoon and wrapped a piece of cloth around the handle and tried to put it in Rab's mouth but his teeth were tightly clenched. Harry didn't persist in trying to insert the spoon because he was aware that more harm than good could be done by trying to force Rab's mouth open. He steadied him to try to prevent him from injuring himself with the convulsive movements.

To me this was a new, frightening experience and I was so relieved there was someone there who knew what to do. After a minute or so the jerking stopped. He appeared to be unconscious but vomited and then slowly woke up, but remained very drowsy. Harry and another of the men helped Rab to his feet and took him to the foreman's office from where they called a taxi to get him home.

Harry later explained to me that this was an epileptic seizure and Rab should never have been on the site because of the dangers working with machinery and working at heights. He hadn't told the foreman about his medical condition when he applied for the job. This incident made me realise how little I knew and ignited a desire to know more.

Mowing a Lawn

One chore I was given on one occasion puzzled me at first. The squad gaffer had disappeared over the lunch break one day and was late coming back, which was very unlike him. When he did come back he appeared, looking rather flushed, from an occupied house close to where we were working. He came back on to the scaffolding and said to me, 'Will you go over to that house there and cut the grass? The poor woman's husband's in prison and she doesn't have anyone to cut it for her.' Always obedient, I trotted off to the very untidy front garden with long grass, where a lawn mower had been left out for me. After cutting the grass I left the mower where I found it and went back to the squad. I never set eyes on the *poor woman* but over the next week or two I noticed some other members of our squad, and indeed of other squads, visiting the same house, and eventually the penny dropped. My cutting the grass had been part payment for services rendered to my gaffer and she had quite a lucrative sideline in the absence of her husband.

Banter

As with any group working together there was a lot of banter between the men and the topics of conversation were often new and alien to me after my narrow up-bringing within a strict evangelical family. Football, the horses, the pub and women were high on the agenda and since some men had been in the war and others had done their National Service afterwards there was a lot of discussion about their exploits when in the forces, including visits to brothels and the signs and symptoms of venereal diseases, STDs as they're now called. There were grossly exaggerated descriptions of the implements and methods used by the medics in investigating and treating the conditions. These included metal hooks being introduced into a certain organ to scrape out samples and the insertion of hot wire to burn and kill the germs.

Drinking alcohol in pubs on a Sunday was not allowed in Scotland at this time, except for bona fide travellers, so the pub landlords got together to get round the law. A landlord in one area would make an arrangement with a landlord in another area at a great enough distance to comply with the law and they would provide a bus to take the customers from Pub A to Pub B, and bring the customers from Pub B to Pub A, thus making them all bona fide travellers. Monday morning chat was all about their weekend drinking exploits.

Gambling was illegal at this time but the men usually played cards for money and the bookie's runner came round every day to take bets for the illegal book-makers who were operating all over the country.

Intellectually they were a very mixed bunch ranging from borderline learning difficulties to those who, given the chance, could have gone on to higher education and university. There were those who could hardly string three words together without swearing and those who spoke very good and polite English; not the stereotypical builder. One bricklayer in our squad was an accomplished ballroom dancer and entered competitions with his wife, his dancing partner. Our annual holiday was one week in July at Glasgow Fair but he always took an extra unpaid week for his dance competitions. Another bricklayer was a member of a choir.

A few were members of the Territorial Army and went off to camp at the holidays and occasionally at weekends. One of the labourers was a military policeman and one Saturday night at one of the camps he had to arrest the gaffer of his own bricklaying squad for being drunk and disorderly. There were some arguments about that when they returned to work.

Some men seemed to spend all their time and money in the pub with no thought for their wives and families and in contrast there were those who were clearly very caring and responsible towards them.

A Labourer Short

With the practice of travelling a distance to drink on Sundays, there was the problem of a busload of men with rapidly filling bladders on the way home. It was common for the driver to have to stop the coach in an isolated spot and they all piled out to relieve themselves by the side of the road.

One Monday morning, Davie, an older labourer who was a regular on these trips, didn't turn up for work. The gaffer asked his pal Tony where he was and Tony replied, 'He's in hospital.'

'What happened?'

'When the coach stopped to let us out for a piss, he couldn't do it. By the time we got back he was in agony, so the driver took him straight to hospital.'

'What did they do?' asked the gaffer, 'do you know if they managed to get rid of it?'

'Yes,' Tam replied. 'They stuck a big tube up his jacksie and attached the other end to a big bottle. He was terrified when he saw the doctor coming with the tube but the result was magic.'

Davie returned to work a week later. They had removed the tube, a catheter, the following day and he was able to pass urine again, but slowly. His prostate was enlarged and he was put on the waiting list to have surgery to widen the narrowed passage through the gland. He didn't go back on the Sunday outings till after his operation.

Faith Challenged

Being exposed to this group of men produced the first challenges to my faith and I began a process of examining and re-examining my beliefs; a spiritual journey which continues to this day. As a child at school I accepted what I was taught, but not without question.

I now found myself having to defend what I believed. Working in Scotland meant quite a lot of time rained off when we were unable to lay bricks, so there were hours spent sitting around in the bothy. Some played cards, some read the papers and some chatted, so they would ask me about my faith and question my beliefs.

The first challenge was to the almost puritanical attitude to *worldly pleasures*. My mother had said to me, 'Remember, if anyone asks why you don't go to the cinema, dancing or football, just say, "It's because I'm a Christian".'

The first time I gave that answer, the next question was, 'So why should being a Christian stop you going to the cinema?' I gave the standard answer which was that cinemas were worldly and Christians could not love the world.

As time went on it became increasingly difficult to be consistent with this argument. Was pleasure itself wrong or was it that certain pleasurable experiences were acceptable while others were unacceptable? One evening at supper our guests, elders and their wives were discussing books they had been reading. One said he had just finished *Gone With the Wind* and my immediate thought was, if it's fine to spend hours reading the book, why is it wrong to see the film? Going to football matches was considered to be wrong but every time there was a church outing of any kind, the first priority for the men was to have the football ready and no matter whether it was the Sunday school, the Bible class or a general church outing there was always a football match.

Later in my apprenticeship I was working with a different squad and the gaffer was also a member of the Christian Brethren. He was very keen on motor sports and went to events as often as possible. I challenged him, pointing out that this was just as worldly as football or cinema. He replied, 'If, as a bricklayer, you were sent to do brickwork at a football or racing stadium, would you do it?' I had no satisfactory answer at that time but gave it serious thought.

I was sixteen and trying to make sense of the long list of Brethren prohibitions. If pleasure itself is not sinful and the means of pleasure are not sinful then the list of activities deemed to be wrong was completely arbitrary. Pleasures involving activities which the Bible deemed to be sinful, such as drunkenness , adultery and gluttony were clearly wrong and the selfish pursuit of a life of self-indulgent pleasure was wrong but gaining pleasure from innocent activities is not the kind of 'worldly pleasure' the Bible condemns.

On another occasion the question of alcohol was raised. Some of the men were heavy drinkers and I had come from a strictly teetotal home, accepting the belief that drinking alcohol was wrong. I was asked, 'Why is drinking alcohol wrong when Jesus and his disciples drank wine? Jesus' first miracle was to turn water into wine at a wedding and he produced the best wine, even when many of the guests were already half drunk.' I had no answer to that but the natural reaction was to try and defend the beliefs I'd had instilled in me.

As on other occasions I gave the challenge serious thought and asked my parents for their opinion at home. This time it exposed a rather odd approach to Biblical interpretation. The Brethren, like other conservative evangelicals, believed the Bible to be the literal, inspired Word of God but my father's answer to my question about alcohol puzzled me. I pointed out, as my workmate had done, that Jesus supplied the wedding guests with wine and that he and his disciples drank wine.

I asked, 'If drinking alcohol is wrong, why did Jesus and his disciples do it?'

My father said, 'Ah well, wine is a symbol of the joy we get from our relationship with Jesus. It's a spiritual lesson for us.'

I replied, 'That may well be true but it doesn't alter the fact that it was real wine he produced and real wine they all drank.' But he just kept repeating the same answer. On looking at the subject for myself I concluded that it is drunkenness that is condemned and not alcohol per se.

This was a boom time in the building industry and there was a fair amount of overtime, which was usually an extra two hours some evenings or Saturday after-noons, paid at time and a half. Sometimes, especially in the winter with dark nights not allowing evening over-time, Sunday shifts were on offer at double time. This was popular with the men but I refused because of my strict Sabbatarian upbringing. This didn't please my gaffer too much because it reduced the amount of bonus the squad could earn. However he did respect my beliefs.

Secret Confession

There were many objections raised to my beliefs and there was a bit of leg-pulling about my faith, but there was a more serious side to some of them in private. At first I didn't know how to react to this because I assumed they were pulling my leg and was a bit defensive.

The first serious encounter was when the gaffer came to me one Monday morning and said, 'I think you're ready to build a corner now. You go and start on that one there and I'll come to see how you're getting on.' The corners are an important part of the building because any mistakes there are carried across the rest of the wall.

The place I was working was a bit away from where the rest of the men were. After I had laid a few courses he came over to me but instead of inspecting my work he said quietly, 'I was at church yesterday.' This was the same gaffer who a few months earlier had asked me to mow a lawn as part payment for the sexual favours he had received from a local prostitute.

Not sure how to react, I replied, 'I hope the roof didn't fall in.'

He looked upset and said, 'No,' in a slow, drawn-out tone that registered his hurt.

I said, 'I'm sorry, Hugh, I'm so used to jokes about Christianity I thought you were joking.'

'No,' he replied, 'it was Communion. My wife goes to church regularly and I always go with her on Communion Sunday.' Communion services in the Church of Scotland tend to be infrequent and it was twice a year at that time.

Hugh went on to explain that their minister held a preparatory service on the Saturday and as a result of that he realised he'd done many things of which he was ashamed. He said, 'I knew I shouldn't take Communion without asking God to forgive me, so I did. Then I was able to take Communion on Sunday with a clear conscience. It feels like a load has been lifted from me.' I was delighted to hear that and told him so, apologising again for my clumsy joke. Then he checked my brickwork which was satisfactory and returned to the rest of the squad.

Say a Prayer

On another occasion when we were rained off, the bothy was full and there were several groups there. Some were playing cards, some were reading newspapers and some were arguing about football. Quite often on those occasions someone would come to me and say, 'Hey, Jimmy, what do you think about . . .?' A discussion on some topic, usually religious would normally follow.

I was reading in a corner when Pat, a labourer came over to me and said quietly, 'Can I speak to you in private?'

'Yes, of course,' I replied, 'we can go over to the navvies' bothy.' Navvies, who did the ground work were supplied with waterproof clothing. They worked in all weathers, so their bothy was empty.

Pat said, 'My wee boy was admitted to hospital yesterday and he's very ill. They don't know what's wrong with him and I'm very worried. I haven't been to church since I was a boy. Will you say a prayer for him?' I assured him I would but he wanted a prayer there and then, so we sat down on the bench and I prayed for young Michael. He remained seriously ill with his life hanging in the balance for a few days. I spoke to Pat most days and assured him of my continued prayers which he said he was grateful for. Then the doctors reached a diagnosis and appropriate treatment was started. Michael gradually recovered.

When I heard the good news I said, 'I'll thank God for Michael's recovery, and it would be nice of you just to say, "Thank you, God".'

He replied, 'No, I thanked the doctors and nurses. They saved him.'

I agreed saying, 'Yes, and you should thank God for their skill and dedication.'

Cycling

When changing buses going to and from Tannochside, I passed a shop that had bicycles in the window. I had loved my little bike when I was much younger so I really wanted one of those bikes in the window. After a few weeks of saving up, now that I was earning I bought one. It was a large upright bicycle with a hub gear and although it wasn't built for speed it was very sturdy and ideal for me at that time. I started cycling to work and to my surprise I discovered that the journey which took well over an hour on the bus could be done in about twenty minutes on the bike by taking a more direct route. This was great, I was saving time and saving money, and I also started shedding the pounds. I'd been very overweight when I started work but the combination of hard physical work and cycling soon corrected that.

The bike became my main interest and I went for long runs in the evenings, on Saturdays and at holiday times. While cycling I met up with two of my old school friends, Beefy and Jim, who were also cycling and we went for runs together. They had sleeker, more light-weight bikes with drop handlebars and derailleur gears which were faster, so I sold my heavy bike and bought a similar bicycle for myself. It made a big difference to my speed.

There was a cycling club in Cambuslang a few miles away and my friends invited me to join. I was very keen till I discovered that most of their activities were on a

Sunday and again my strict Sabbatarian principles put a stop to that.

Darkness

I gradually extended my cycling distance and went for fairly long runs. On my first New Year's Day after leaving school I cycled to Lanark and from there to Abington, and then turned back along the A74 towards home, a round trip of about eighty-five miles. It must have been around 5 pm as I was leaving Abington to do the final thirty-six-mile leg of the journey home and it was dark by then. It had mainly been a bright sunny day but now there were thick clouds and it was starting to rain. Very soon I was on a fifteen-mile stretch of isolated unlit road in pitch darkness crossing the Douglas Moor. Normally this was a busy carriageway, being the main road between Glasgow and London, but since it was New Year's Day there was almost no traffic. I had a terrible feeling of isolation and just a little fear as I cycled through the darkness remembering the Wanlockhead tales of Burke and Hare and the Covenanters.

There was an isolated cottage on the moor and when I came to it I decided enough was enough, so I went and knocked on the door. It looked rather creepy and dimly lit but a man answered and opened the door just a few inches. He looked more scared than I was but asked what I wanted. Not wanting to admit to being a bit afraid I said I was cycling home but was tired and asked him to keep my bike for me so that I could hitch a lift home. He wisely reminded me that it was New Year and there was almost no traffic on the road so I should persevere, and he pointed out that just a few miles further on the road started to go downhill and it would be much easier. I thanked him and asked for a drink of water and then continued on my way, feeling less isolated for having spoken to a human being. Eventually the first sign of street lights appeared and the dark areas became shorter with the lights of scattered rural villages visible in the distance.

As I entered Larkhall about twelve miles from home my front light went out and I didn't have a replacement bulb. Being New Year's Day, the highest and holiest day of the year in Scotland, and evening, there were no shops open where I could buy a replacement or even a small torch so I got off my bike and started walking because cycling at night without a front and back light was illegal. For some reason I had an excessively strong respect for the law. So I walked, pushing my bike all the way home.

Why on earth I didn't chance it and cycle most of the way I don't know, since much of my route from there had street lights. As a result I arrived home about 2 am to frantic parents who were imagining all sorts of things. My father had gone to the police station to ask about any reports of accidents and used a telephone call box to ring round various hospitals to see if I'd been taken there. In those days very few working-class people had telephones and I didn't know of any neighbours who had one so there was no way I could have let them know I was fine.

I vowed then that I wouldn't go out on long stretches of dark unlit roads any more. However it wasn't long before I was at it again. On one evening it was dark and misty so shapes and sizes were distorted as I cycled over Eaglesham Moor. As I was going uphill I saw a shape in front of me. It was huge and looked like a monster but as I got closer I thought, no, it must be a horse, then nearer still I thought, no, it's just a cow, and then lo and behold when I was quite close the monster had turned into a sheep.

Getting caught out like this happened to me many times, such as when I came back along the A8 from the East Coast, or down the Firth of Clyde lochs, always because I underestimated how early darkness would fall. Each time it happened I vowed I would never do it again and even decided to get rid of my bike to stop myself, but never did. Cycling was the great love of my life at that time.

I had enjoyed cycling with my friends from school and made some new friends in the building industry, but one of the problems associated with growing up in, and being a member of a narrow religious denomination is that you gradually lose contact with old friends. It also becomes extremely difficult to make new, lasting friendships outside the church. Their interests and activities were not compatible with the unremitting 'Thou shalt not' approach of the Brethren. As a result most of my cycling was on my own but I enjoyed my own company and never felt lonely.

Later in my early twenties when opportunities for cycling became fewer, I looked back nostalgically at that time and composed a poem, *My bike and I.*

Image 6-2: Footbridge over Clyde at David Livingstone Centre between Blantyre and Bothwell

My Bike and I
On leaving school I thought I'd like
To go to work, so bought a bike,
When I was fifteen years of age
And old enough to earn a wage.

My desire was to learn to build,
So leaving Blantyre, still unskilled,
I went towards the River Clyde,
Down the hill to the river side,

Where David Livingstone was born,
Then o'er the footbridge every morn'.
Onward I climbed the other side
And made my way to Tannochside,

Where building work had just begun.
I worked o'er there till day was done,
Came back home a similar way,
My bike and I each working day.

To me my bike became a friend.
More time together we would spend,
When not at work and free to go
Where e're we wanted, to and fro'.

Going across the Fenwick Moor,
Reaching the Ayrshire coast was sure.
Wind in my face or at my back
We went far off the beaten track,

Travelling through the countryside,
Keeping close to the River Clyde,
On to Lanark tracing its course,
Into the hills to seek its source.

On again to reach Wanlockhead
High in the Lowther Hills ahead
Where lead was mined in years gone by,
Now gold is panned; well worth a try.

The firth of Clyde; a sight to see,
As river merges with the sea,
A place my bike and I could go
To feel the gentle breezes blow.

We watched as many sailed their yachts,
And on we went with happy thoughts
To visit Gare Loch and Loch Long,
Then over land humming a song,

To the loch by yon bonnie braes,
Loch Lomond where we'd stop and gaze,
Then cycle by its bonnie banks
To go back home, heart full of thanks.

Racing my bike was not for me,
But touring Scotland roaming free,
Exploring every country lane,
In sunshine, wind and even rain.

From Blantyre down to Gretna Green,
Or going north to Aberdeen,
We saw so many Scottish towns,
And heard so many country sounds.

That freedom with my two wheeled friend
Is something I can recommend,
And many more should really try
The joy we had, my bike and I.

The Scotts Again

In the early years of my apprenticeship there were no other young men of a similar age in the local Brethren Church so I tended to go there with other family members or alone. Step in the Scotts again. As I said before Aunt Jenny was very kind but tended to dominate the other two sisters. Aunt Jenny and Uncle George came up with a plan for me. Uncle George took every second Saturday afternoon off and often went on bus tours. I was invited to join him but didn't really know whether it was intended as company for me or for him, but I went along. On the first occasion it went well and we chatted about what we were seeing and doing.

But Uncle George was a moody man and on the second occasion he was sullen and silent for most of the journey, making it very uncomfortable. How I wished I was out on my bike enjoying my own company with the wind in my face! I never repeated the experience.

There was another occasion when the Scotts decided I should have company. My cousin Walter, who was no longer my foreman, was going to Wanlockhead for the weekend with his wife May. He had a Ford Popular car and I was invited to join them. I always enjoyed Wanlockhead and accepted the invitation looking forward to doing some hillwalking there, but we weren't long on the journey before I realised I'd made a mistake. I felt trapped sitting in the back of a car when I could have been out in the open air on my bike. In addition May was sulky and often silent which added to my misery. On arrival at Aunt Jean's house I learned why. May was in the early stages of pregnancy with her first child and the reason for the trip was to let Aunt Jean know. However, after this enough was enough and I firmly declined any other offers of company.

A Family Row

The family might have felt I needed the company but I certainly didn't. I was perfectly happy on my own or with other apprentices with whom I sometimes went on cycling tours. This of course may have been the motivation for the family trying to get company for me. Keeping company socially with people outside the Brethren was frowned on because of the fear that these worldly friends might entice us away from the church.

My sister Isabel, who was three years older than I, was very unhappy with the lack of company, especially the lack of opportunity to meet male company of her own age. One Sunday after we returned home from the morning service we sat round the small table in the kitchen for lunch as usual and Isabel, then aged nineteen, said, 'I've had enough of this, I'm not going back to church. I intend to get out into the world and meet people and enjoy myself a bit.'

My father said, 'If you do that, you can get out of this house. You'll no longer be welcome here.'

I could see the shocked look on my mother's face but before she could react, I did, and my pent-up frustration with his apparent lack of interest in us erupted. I told him in no uncertain terms what I thought of his gospel preaching about God's love and patience towards sinners, his preaching that people can come to Christ freely for forgiveness and that God forces no one, but here he was trying to force his daughter into his straitjacket.

I finished off with, 'You've no moral authority to try to force her in this way and if she leaves we all leave. After all, you've never shown any interest in your family growing up except in relation to your precious church.' He looked shocked for a moment and then came up with his usual defence; that he was called to preach the gospel but had always provided for us.

I'd recently read a book about the exploits of a foreign missionary and noted that he always set aside time every day to spend with his family and play with his children. I pointed this out to my father, but of course I overlooked the fact that there were other missionaries with the opposite approach. David Livingstone, one of my heroes, was one who neglected his wife and family and they didn't see him for years on end. The row passed and things continued as before, at least on the surface, but I was surprised at myself and felt extremely guilty at my reaction. I did apologise later for my outburst and said it had been in the heat of the moment in defence of my sister.

Not long after this some other young people, male and female, joined the church and Isabel had the company she longed for. I too had three new friends, Simon, Sam and Joe, within the church. They'd just completed their Military National Service and come to work in the area. Simon was working as a gardening assistant at the local Hairmyres Hospital, Sam as an operative in a sewage works and Joe as a building labourer. They didn't cycle much so I was still able to enjoy that activity on my own especially the long runs.

Stoneymeadow

We became good friends and went on walks or did some cycling together but only short runs within a few miles of home. One favourite run was to head towards East Kilbride and through the hamlet of Stoneymeadow. There was a small shop and petrol pump there, run by a very pleasant old gentleman, Mr Philips. He sold soft drinks and cold snacks. We often stopped there to have a drink and a snack before going on to cycle around the network of farm roads in the area. Wagon Wheels chocolate biscuits were our favourite snacks.

Observing Mr Philips at the petrol pump was fascinating. Fortunately he wasn't very busy but when a car drew up for petrol he came out with a marked limp, and a walking stick in one hand. Leaning his stick on the pump, he put the nozzle in the car with one hand and put the other hand on a lever on the side of the pump. Then he proceeded to pull and push the lever to manually pump the petrol into the car. He had no electricity supply.

After serving his customer he often sat with us on the bench in front of the shop and chatted to us about life in general, telling us tales of times gone by. We always enjoyed his company and I think he ours.

School of Building

The company I was working for was Weir Housing Corporation based in Coatbridge, and they participated in a scheme for training apprentices. This involved us going to a college or school of building once a week on day release during college term time. It was compulsory for the first three years, so I enrolled at Cambuslang School of Building. The bricklaying section was later moved to an annexe in Blantyre a short walk from home, which suited me perfectly.

It was not long before I realised that the highlight of my week was my day at the School of Building, partly because I didn't need to get up so early in the morning but mainly because I was enjoying studying and learning. Having spent my three years of secondary education looking forward to the day I could leave school and start work, I now spent my working days looking forward to my day at school.

Our general science course at school had concentrated more on physics and chemistry and my memory of biology was mainly about flowers and insects. I knew nothing of the workings of the human body. During our first term at the School of Building we were taught first aid and although this concentrated on those aspects of anatomy related to accidents such as bones, main blood vessels and breathing apparatus, it opened a whole new world to me and made me determined to learn more. I recalled the incident with the epileptic and although it had nothing to do with accidents, it was an incident requiring first aid, so I asked the lecturer about it. He said, 'This isn't something you should encounter because people subject to seizures should not be working on building sites,' but he helpfully gave a brief outline of a grand mal seizure and how to deal with it.

After the three compulsory years at the School of Building we sat the Intermediate City and Guilds examination in Bricklaying, and those who passed and wanted to could continue the day release for a further two years to sit the Final City and Guilds examination. I passed comfortably and continued the day release for the next two years to gain the Final City and Guilds Certificate in Bricklaying. During my final two years I also enrolled for night classes to do two nights per week for the Ordinary National Certificate in Building Technology.

Skills learned on the job were basic bricklaying skills used in council housing building schemes. More specialised building techniques plus some maths, science and regulations related to building were learned at the School of Building.

Musical?

I was restless and always looking for ways to improve myself, so I decided to learn to play the piano. Like so much of the furniture from the tenement the old pedal organ was infested with woodworm and had to be thrown out. Our parents acquired a second-hand piano to replace it. Isabel, who had been able to play the organ by ear from childhood, was now learning to read music and play properly, but I didn't want to go to a teacher so I enrolled for a distance learning course. It was called *The Graphonote System* and used a diagram of the piano keyboard alongside the text. This wasn't very satisfactory so I gave up, and then when chatting with one of my workmates he told me he played the accordion. I liked the sound of that so I bought one, but this time I realised I needed a teacher so enrolled with the same teacher as Isabel.

This worked and I enjoyed it, making fairly good progress and learning some good tunes at a basic level but my progress was slow, mainly because I didn't practise enough and probably because I didn't have the aptitude for more than the basics, so I gave up after a year or so.

Linen

When I was in the second year of my apprenticeship my father wanted a shed in the back garden so I built one of brick and put a reinforced concrete roof on it. He was a handy man and of course had worked for many years as a bricklayers' labourer so he put in the door and window. My younger brother, John, became an apprentice joiner later but he was still at school.

I had no knowledge of building regulations at this time, and a year or so after completing the shed we received a letter from Building Control pointing out the error of our ways. They informed us that we had built a permanent structure without planning permission and would be getting a visit from one of their officials. Apparently a kind neighbour had reported us to the council. Although they wouldn't say who had reported us we had a strong suspicion. A close neighbour was a very jealous man and had already reported someone else for a minor infringement of the regulations. The officer who came was pleasant and helpful but informed us that it was larger than what was allowed without permission, so we would have to apply for retrospective planning permission.

We sent for the necessary papers and when they arrived John and I read the instructions carefully. Plans, drawn to scale, had to be submitted on linen.

'Linen!' we said, 'what's wrong with paper?' We had no idea what they meant so we went to Mum and asked for a piece of linen. Always willing to help she cut up an old tablecloth and I got out my drawing board, T-square and set squares, and set about producing the necessary scale drawings on my mother's old tablecloth. They must have had a right good laugh in the Planning Department and it probably put them in a good mood because it did the trick and we got our retrospective planning permission. The *linen* referred to is a high quality paper reinforced with linen fibres and was essential for any legal document at that time. We did learn about dealing with authorities later in the building course.

Nomad

Bricklaying was a fairly nomadic existence with workers being paid off at the end of a job and having to move to another site somewhere else. I started at Tannochside, Uddingston and was there for about a year. When that housing scheme was completed our squad was sent to Slamanan in Stirlingshire for a few months to finish off a scheme there. Each time we moved we had a different foreman so I no longer had contact with my cousin. Not that he showed me any favours, but he was probably quietly looking out for me.

Slamanan involved three buses each way and meant me leaving the house at 6 am to get there for 8. There was no shortcut for the bike; cycling there would have taken considerably longer. From there we went to Muirkirk and then to New Cumnock in Ayrshire.

These were interesting journeys. The company put on a lorry with a *cape* on the back from Coatbridge to take the men there and back daily. A cape was a sort of simple shed with seats but no floor and only an opening for a door, which sat on the back of the lorry. The only thing holding it down was the weight of the men sitting on the seats. It is unlikely that Health and Safety would allow such means of transport now.

I took a bus to Hamilton and boarded the lorry there. It was very cold especially in the winter and we devised various methods to keep us warm. Some took hot-water bottles on the way to work and heated bricks on the bothy stove for the journey home. Hot Bovril or Oxo in flasks became very popular among the men.

Unclean, Unclean

Having grown up in an evangelical Christian environment, I was familiar with the Bible stories about the treatment and isolation of people with leprosy, and how they had to call out, 'Unclean, unclean,' to keep others away from them. One day when we were at Muirkirk we were a labourer short and as the youngest apprentice I was sent to help. I was given the job of mixing mortar. In the process I managed to get myself covered in dry cement.

The following morning I noticed a couple of small spots on my face and thought this must be irritation due to the cement but by lunchtime it had spread across my face and one of the men said, 'You have impetigo and it's highly contagious, you need to get off the site right away.'

I said, 'I can't go, I have to wait for the lorry to take us home.' By this time his anxiety had spread to the others and I was ordered off the site immediately. There was no way they were going to allow me to travel in the cape on the back of a lorry to Hamilton.

I returned to the scaffolding and gathered my tools to clean them and put them away then headed for the road. Hamilton was more than thirty miles from Muirkirk and half of that was over the rather desolate Muirkirk Moor. Fortunately it wasn't raining and I set off on foot, trying to thumb a lift as I went. Drivers generally ignored me but after I'd walked about two miles a van driver stopped and offered me a lift. I assume he didn't recognise the rash as being significant but I was very grateful to him. He took me to Hamilton where I was able to get the bus home.

The following morning I went to see my GP, Dr Gordon. There were no appointments in those days. You just went and sat in the queue. He confirmed that I did have impetigo and it was very contagious. A course of antibiotic cream cleared it up over several days and I was able to go back to work without carrying my placard marked 'Unclean'.

Turning an Eyelid

Cutting bricks with a brick hammer was a normal part of bricklaying, as was trimming off rough edges with a *scutch*, a type of hammer or chisel with a serrated edge. These activities resulted in small pieces of brick flying off and since goggles were never used, a foreign body in the eye was an occasional injury. A skill passed on by some was the ability to *look an eye* or *turn an eyelid* to remove the fragment of brick. A matchstick was obtained and placed at the top of the upper eyelid. The eyelashes were grasped and the eyelid lifted to turn it inside out over the matchstick. Then the corner of a not very clean handkerchief was used to remove the foreign body. Some were very skilled at this and it was rarely necessary to call for medical help.

Further Travels and Increasing Experience

There followed housing schemes in Wishaw, Newarthill and East Kilbride new town, all in Lanarkshire, during which time I increased my speed and experience. During my time in East Kilbride I spend some months working on my own doing what we called *jobbing* which I think is now called *snagging*. Holes were left in walls for plumbing pipes and these had to be filled in after the plumber had done his work. Windows had to be pointed to make the edges watertight after the joiners fitted them and internal walls had channels cut in them to allow electricians to put in metal conduits for their cables.

After homes were allocated, the new occupants could go to the Master of Works with any complaints they had. I was given the job of investigating any complaints related to brickwork. On one occasion I was sent to see an irate lady who was complaining about her chimney. She had lit her fire and the smoke bellowed out into the room making her new walls and furniture sooty. I put a rod up the chimney and it went no further than about four feet. So I scaled the roof and lowered a metal ball on a rope but again it went no further than what I estimated to be about halfway down her living room wall. This would be just about level with the top of the bend. Domestic chimneys don't go straight up from the fireplace but at an angle of about 45° for the first few feet.

I broke through the wall and into the chimney just above the blockage to the smell of decomposing flesh.

Shining a torch I discovered a dead seagull lying on top of two bricks and a pile of hard mortar. When I told my foreman about it and asked if he knew who had built the chimney, he said, 'I don't know but I'll find out.' At the end of the week when I was collecting my pay packet he said, 'I know what happened. I sacked a bricklayer who was in the squad working on that block and before he left apparently he threw two bricks and a bucket of mortar down the chimney.' It must have stuck at the bend and at a later date the unfortunate gull must have fallen down and been unable to escape.

Family Finances

My father had continued to work as a bread salesman with Welma Bakeries. He delivered the bread, which he carried on a board on his head. At the end of each week he was responsible for collecting the money from the shops for the bread he'd sold. Sometimes the figures on the sales slips didn't match the money collected and he spent hours going through the figures again and again. In most cases it was a clerical error on his part but occasionally they couldn't be reconciled and he had to make up any discrepancy from his wages.

While I was working in East Kilbride a friend of the family recommended a new job to Dad. It was with Sistacream, a new company that made synthetic cream and they were looking for salesmen to go round shops promoting and selling their products. He applied and was accepted for the job which he thoroughly enjoyed at first. He drove all over Lanarkshire in their van promoting the new products and was doing well but there was trouble ahead. Political problems in the Middle East resulted in a petrol shortage and the company couldn't get enough fuel for his extensive travels, so his journeys were limited to the local area.

This resulted in considerable loss of income and financial difficulties for the family, and sometimes there was no money to pay bills due on a Friday. He'd come to East Kilbride on a Friday at lunchtime just as I'd been paid and I handed my wages over. This clearly couldn't go on so he approached his former employer to see if they had any vacancies. Fortunately his old run in the Gorbals had gone downhill since he left and they welcomed him back.

A Girlfriend

Having been brought up in a Christian home and being taught the Christian faith there was never a time when I didn't accept it, so when I was about sixteen I was baptised and became a member of the Brethren in Bethany Hall, Blantyre. Brethren, like Baptists, do not practise infant baptism but instead baptise adults by total immersion when the candidates are able to understand what they're doing.

After leaving Sunday school we went to Bible class and one annual event was the Bible class social. This, like the Sunday school soirée, was a Christian concert with invited singers such as soloists and groups, and we, the

Bible class, formed a choir. There was a meal and of course the inevitable speaker with a message to try to make converts from among the guests.

It was at one such social when I was seventeen and there was a group singing, the Cambuslang Ladies Trio. The youngest member was a lovely redhead, Mary Wilson, who caught my eye immediately, and we got chatting afterwards and agreed to a date. We had a couple of dates and then her mother put a stop to it because she said Mary was too young, at fifteen. However, a year later, through the matchmaking efforts of my brother John, we met up again and started seeing each other regularly.

One of the big problems associated with our puritanical lifestyle was what to do and where to go when going out as a couple. Cinema, theatre, dancing and spectator sports were not allowed, so where could we go? Generally we went for walks, took bus runs to the coast or country, or sat in and listened to the radio. Although there was no radio in our home, Mary's parents did have a radio for limited use so we could listen to that and we enjoyed Saturday Night Theatre. Some weekends we went, along with other family and friends, to stay with Aunt Jean in Wanlockhead to do some hill-walking or just general larking around.

There were special young people's services organised by the Brethren hierarchy on Saturday evenings in Glasgow and many went there and then met up for a chat and whatever else in a tearoom afterwards. Before we met, Mary had associations with the Tent Hall, a large interdenominational mission in Glasgow's Saltmarket and we went to the services there some Saturday evenings.

Mary didn't have a bicycle and wasn't interested in cycling so dates never included my bike. She lived in Rutherglen close to the boundary with Cambuslang and the family went to church in Cambuslang. I took the bus to Cambuslang and Mary met me at the bus stop or I walked the half mile to her home. When we returned after our time out we said goodnight at the foot of the stairs inside her front door. However, after a few weeks we were allowed to use her bedroom, and were never disturbed no matter how long we were there, apart from once. This always surprised me because Mary's mother, another Mary, was very Victorian. Perhaps it was because she liked and trusted me. Oh dear!

Mary's dad, Roddy, worked in the steelworks and when he was on night shift he left about 9 pm to get there early for starting at 10. One evening his jacket was in the room we were using and he tried to walk into the room to get it, but we had a chair against the door. Although we had never been disturbed we didn't take any chances. As a result he had to wait a few minutes till we got up off the floor and made the appropriate adjustments. He was none too pleased.

My time was limited by the last bus. It usually went about 10.30 pm and, since it was difficult for us to pull ourselves away from each other, I always left it till the last minute and ran the half mile to catch the bus. I frequently missed it and had to walk the five miles home to Blantyre. Occasionally a kind man in an old Austin 8 car, with a hole in the floor and pigeon baskets in the back, would stop and give me a lift part of the way. I was always delighted to see him.

Elderly Relatives

A year or so into my apprenticeship Dad had a phone call from a neighbour of Uncle Willie's in Langholm. His Parkinson's disease had progressed and he wasn't coping on his own. Arrangements were made for him to be brought to Blantyre to stay with us but this wasn't ideal. We didn't have a spare room and he couldn't manage the stairs in any case. Fortunately the bathroom was down-stairs so a folding bed was put in the living room.

It was an awkward arrangement with teenagers in the house and we were grumpy about the lack of freedom especially after he went to bed at night. However after six months or so his affairs in Langholm were settled, and Mum's home cooking and TLC got his health to a much better condition. Being more mobile and clearer men-tally he found what was the 1950s equivalent of sheltered housing. He rented a ground-floor room in a block of flats with a caretaker and a main meal provided each day. This worked well for him and we were able to visit and keep an eye on things.

My paternal grandmother lived in a first-floor tene-ment flat in High Blantyre and we visited her and she us on occasions. As with most tenements it was becoming unfit for habitation and she became too frail to manage the stairs.

She had to be rehoused but no suitable house could be found so she too came to live with us for a time. This was about a year after Uncle Willie left us and there was the same problem with sleeping arrangements but we still had the extra folding bed in the living room. Fortunately after four or five months a suitable house on the ground floor was found just a few streets away.

Because she was now frail and in the early stage of dementia she required a lot of supervision so we all took it in turn to visit three times a day. Mum got her up in the morning and gave her breakfast. Dad went in at teatime while out preaching and Mum went in with Isabel, John or me to settle her for the night.

She had three daughters but two were too far away to help. One lived in rural Argyll and one in Portsmouth. The third, Aunt Maisie, was now living in Hamilton five miles away and she helped out whenever possible. This continued for about two years and then one night in 1957 when Mum and I went to see her at 8pm she was complaining of chest pain. She was pale and clammy and memories of Uncle Tom rang alarm bells so we called the doctor. He arrived in about half an hour and after examining her said, 'She's had a heart attack and needs to go into hospital.' He arranged her admission and called an ambulance but sadly she died before it arrived.

Military Service?

After World War II until 1960, young men between the ages of eighteen and twenty-five were required to do a period of National Service. This was for eighteen months at first but increased to two years. Students and those doing apprenticeships were allowed to defer this until the training was complete, so I was allowed to defer for two years till my apprenticeship was completed, but this concentrated my mind on my attitudes to military service, war and killing.

Decision

The Brethren didn't have a fixed position on Christians and war, so it was left to each to decide according to their beliefs and conscience. I knew some who had done their military service and some who were conscientious objectors, but I was not aware of any ill feeling between the two groups. Each appeared to respect the other's beliefs.

The strongest influence on me towards a pacifist position was from my father, who was strongly anti-military, and had objected to me being in the Boy Scouts on the grounds that it was preparation for military service. Mary's brother Willie who was two years older than I had been a conscientious objector, and I worked with a joiner, on a building site near the end of my apprenticeship, who was also a member of the Christian Brethren and he too had conscientious objections. On the other hand I had friends in the local church who had recently completed their National Service. Although each was convinced that his decision was the correct one neither group, apart from my father, tried to influence me.

I determined to use those two years to study the different arguments and read books by opposing writers. By the end of the two years I'd decided that I must object on the grounds of conscience. The point of no return came when we had to go to the local Labour Exchange, equivalent to the Jobcentre Plus now, and register for military service. I remember standing at the desk and the man asking me a lot of questions such as my name, address, date of birth, present occupation and about my health. Then he came to the question, 'Which of the services would you prefer?'

I said, 'I'm a conscientious objector.'

He was furious, saying, 'Why didn't you tell me that earlier? I need different forms for people like you.' He tore up the form and stormed off. I thought I must have seriously upset him and was wondering what to do. Leaving wasn't an option so I just had to wait until he returned, grumbling, with the relevant forms.

Tribunal

Following this I had to wait for a citation to appear before a tribunal to be examined for them to decide if they thought my objections were truly on the grounds of conscience or if I was *a skiver, or draft-dodger*. I was sent paperwork to complete and had to send in a statement outlining the reasons for my objections, which I assumed would form the basis of their questioning.

Many working-class people around Glasgow and Lanarkshire had a habit of mispronouncing and misspelling the word *identified*. In my statement I made reference to being identified with the Prince of Peace. After completing the statement I gave it to my father for his comments. He said, 'It's fine but you made a spelling mistake. You've written "identified" but it should be "indentified".' I tried to argue with him but he insisted. Unfortunately we didn't have a dictionary in the house, so I rewrote it with his spelling.

The tribunals, so far as I'm aware, were made up of a military expert, a religious expert and, I think, a legal or knowledgeable lay person. They had four possible decisions: 1. Place the applicant unconditionally on the Register of Conscientious Objectors; 2. Place him on the Register with conditions; 3. Register him for military service as a non-combatant or 4. Reject the application and require him to do the full military service. This last decision left the objector with the choice of doing National Service or going to prison.

In due course I received my citation. I was allowed to take a representative, either legal or religious, but decided that it was *my* conscience that was being examined and I should speak for myself. Since my father was working, Mary's father came along with me for moral support but sat at the back of the room. There were three of us being examined and we all sat in the same room with three examiners sitting at a table in front of us. I was the last to be interviewed so heard the full proceedings for the other two.

A Baptist

The first was a Baptist who made a bit of a mess of his defence. He did have a representative with him but he simply gave a character reference. This objector had not applied to be registered as a conscientious objector at the normal time but did so later, so they questioned him rather aggressively on this. He said he'd been training for the Baptist ministry and would have had automatic exemption from military service as a minister, but had married during the course and was forced to leave the Baptist College.

This meant he was required to do his National Service but since he objected to military service on the grounds of conscience he had to apply for registration later than usual. There was some very stern questioning on whether Baptists required their ministers to be celibate and he was a bit evasive but eventually said, 'No, they don't.'

At one point he appeared to misunderstand a question and laughed a little when his error was pointed out. One member of the tribunal told him off in no uncertain manner, pointing out that he was an educated man and should have known better.

After further questioning and his trying to skirt around the questions the truth came out. He had been training for the Baptist ministry but got his girlfriend pregnant and was expelled from the college. I don't think he was questioned much on his reasons for objecting to military service after that, but his application was rejected and he was ordered to do the full National Service.

A Jehovah's Witness

The second young man also had a representative with him but he had an easier time. He was a Jehovah's Witness and objected to killing or being trained to kill but had no objections to military service in a non-combatant role. Unlike Brethren and Baptists, Jehovah's Witnesses had a firm position on military service. There were some questions about how long he had been a Jehovah's Witness and how he came to join the church, followed by some basic questions about his objections to killing.

They said, 'Surely the Bible is against murder rather than against necessary killing in war?' As is usually the case with Jehovah's Witnesses, he was well primed and well rehearsed. He gave firm, assured answers and they agreed to his doing National Service as a non-combatant.

My Turn

Then came my turn! The first question was why didn't I have a representative. I said that as it was my conscience and beliefs that were being tested I should speak for myself. In retrospect I think this was naive and I may have had an easier time if I'd at least taken an elder as a character witness and to confirm my lifelong association with the Christian Brethren. Rather than using my written statement as the basis for questioning, they asked some in-depth questions about my parents and upbringing. Were my parents in the Brethren? Was my father in the forces? How and why did he come to join the Brethren? How and why did my mother come to join?

Then they came to some of the more esoteric beliefs held among the Brethren but by no means universally agreed by them. I was asked if the place I worked was a closed shop. This was not a term I was familiar with so I replied, 'No, I work outside on building sites.'

They looked at each other and smiled and the questioner said, 'No, I mean does everyone have to be a member of the trade union?' At this point I allowed myself a smile, but remembering how annoyed they'd been at the first person's reaction to a misunderstanding, I quickly became serious again.

I was asked if I was a member of a trade union and I said, 'No, but I was recently approached and told I must join, but I refused. The foreman was sent by the shop steward to tell me it was my duty to join and there could be trouble if I didn't. I went to the shop steward and explained my position to him and said that I was going before a tribunal but whatever the outcome I would be off his site within a few weeks. He was happy to leave it at that.'

When this was explained to the tribunal they moved on to the next line of questioning.

'Do you vote in elections?'

I said that I did not. My reason for this was based on a rather vague understanding, or misunderstanding, of Nebuchadnezzar's dream in the book of Daniel in the Old Testament. Nebuchadnezzar and his empire were described as the head of gold in a dream about a great statue and each successive empire became less valuable and less strong. Coupled with this, there were Samuel's objections to Israel wanting a king, theocracy being God's way and democracy being the poorest and weakest of all systems of government. I had not been prepared for this line of questioning and fumbled in my answers. One of them said, 'Well, who would arrange things like emptying the bins, cleaning the streets and paying for water supplies and so forth?'

I said, 'The local council would,' but wasn't given a chance to explain my reasoning.

Then they asked me if there was anything else I wanted to say in defence of my objections, so I highlighted the points I had made in my written statement and which they'd ignored in the hearing so far. Hearing the Jehovah's Witness defend his objections to killing but his willingness to be part of the armed forces in a non-combatant role I felt the need to explain why I was not willing to serve as a non-combatant. I think I said something like, 'Being a non-combatant would still make me part of the whole military machine and it would be inconsistent of me to refuse to kill but do work that enables others to kill.'

They adjourned to consider their decision and came back after about ten minutes. I was accepted for conditional registration on the Register of Conscientious Objectors. The condition was that, for a period of two years and three months, I must work in one of a number of occupations deemed to be of national importance, one of which was hospital work.

At this time I was working alongside a joiner who'd been before a tribunal a couple of years earlier and informed me that he had argued that the building industry was work of national importance, and was allowed to continue in his trade. However, prior to my appearance before the tribunal I'd been visiting our local Hairmyres Hospital along with Isabel. As we approached a main corridor I saw two young men in white coats coming out. They were not the usual white coats worn by doctors but went up to the neck like a clerical collar and one had blue epaulettes on the shoulders. I asked Isabel, 'Are they doctors?'

'No,' she replied, 'they're male nurses.'

I said, 'I didn't know men could be nurses.'

'Oh yes, there are several in this hospital,' she continued.

As result of examining my conscience and beliefs regarding military service I felt God was calling me to care for the sick; to heal rather than kill. I couldn't be a doctor but perhaps I could be a nurse.

Reactions

Reactions to me when I made my conscientious objections known were mixed among my workmates and fellow students at the School of Building. Some of my workmates had served during the Second World War, some were members of the Territorial Army and the rest had done their National Service. They all profoundly disagreed with me, but while some respected my position many were hostile. One was sarcastic, saying with a serious face and phony sympathetic voice, 'I'll be a conscientious objector too if there's another war.'

When I asked him what the grounds for his objections were he said, 'I don't see why I should have to go and fight for my country when people like you can say you object and get away with it.'

Towards the end of our final year at the School of Building we had a visit from an inspector. He didn't do much inspecting in terms of our building knowledge or skills but decided to ask us all which of the military services we were going to do our National Service in, then have a discussion on general knowledge. When my turn came I said I was a conscientious objector.

Most of the other students kept quiet but a few were openly hostile. The main reason for their hostility was the belief that, having now completed our apprenticeships, and being at the stage when we could earn good money, they had to go off to do National Service but I could continue in my trade and earn the higher wages. However I pointed out that I was expecting to go into nursing training and as a student nurse would be getting less than they, and while their National Service would last two years my conditions committed me to two years and three months. The full training, however, was for three years and I intended to complete it. This all took up a large part of the inspector's discussion time. The second part of the discussion was about Britain's attack on the Suez Canal.

In 1956 President Nasser of Egypt nationalised the Suez Canal Company, which was run by France with Britain as the largest shareholder. Although this nationalisation was legal in international law it worried France and Britain because Egypt sided with Russia in the Cold War, and Britain and France needed the Canal for access to oil supplies in the Gulf, and for access to their empires. A plan was hatched for Israel to attack the Canal and then for Britain and France to come in as peacekeepers. Israel duly attacked but when President Nasser didn't submit to the peacekeeping plan, Britain, under Prime Minister Antony Eden, bombed them. Most of the world, including the USA, was against this action.

We were to be divided into two groups, one group to argue in favour of the invasion and the other against. The inspector said to me, 'I'm sorry if this puts you in the position of having to argue for war but it's only an exercise, and the whole point is so we can see both sides of the argument.' As it so happened I was in the group who had to argue against the invasion so I was able present some of my objections to war.

Throughout my adult life, starting with my discussions with my workmates, I've always tried to be intellectually honest, and if I've been swayed by an argument I'll carefully examine both sides and seek the truth rather than try to defend my belief system. As a result my beliefs have evolved over the years and this is also true of my beliefs regarding war, trade unions and democracy. I still find war abhorrent but fully accept that nations have a right to defend themselves and in some cases to defend others who are being oppressed. I now accept the concept of the *just war,* but deciding what is a just war and what is not is a perennial problem. Democracy, with non-compulsory trade unions, is similarly an essential part of a free and fair society.

Chapter 7

Nursing at Hairmyres Hospital

Interviews

After receiving the decision of the tribunal I went along to the local Labour Exchange and said, 'I have to get work in a hospital as a male nurse.'

The man there said, 'You mean you would *like* to work in a hospital.'

'No,' I replied, 'I *have* to work in a hospital,' and he repeated his comment.

So I explained my situation and he telephoned Hairmyres Hospital there and then and gave me a time and a date to go for an interview with the comment, 'These people are very busy so don't muck them about, make sure you go and arrive on time.' He gave me an application form to complete and take with me to the interview. On this occasion as on others I was very naive regarding the use of referees. I gave two of my friends as referees. Simon had recently started working as a gardening assistant in the hospital grounds and Joe was a building labourer; surely two of the most qualified people to vouch for me as a potential nurse! The matron was Miss Hardie and on arrival I was ushered into her

185

office where she asked a lot of questions. Three stand out. The first was about my reasons for wanting to train as a nurse, and why I was leaving the building industry, since she like most people thought changing from bricklaying to nursing was a very big cultural jump. This led me to explain my conscientious objections to military service, and that didn't go down too well with her, as with many I met during my training.

She looked me straight in the eye and said, 'I profoundly disagree with you but you're entitled to your opinion.' What I was to learn very soon was that most of the more experienced nurses and tutors had nursed during the war and had witnessed the horrendous injuries many of our soldiers, sailors and airmen had suffered in defending us and fighting against the evil Nazi empire.

The second question was about my referees and Matron asked me if I knew anyone in nursing in the hospital for another reference. I said, 'No,' but in fact I had a relative through marriage, Isabel Young, who was also a member of the Brethren in Bethany Hall, Blantyre. She was a theatre sister and would have been an ideal referee but somehow I didn't think of her because I didn't know her very well. A pity, because since she was Uncle George's niece and therefore from the Scott side of the family, Aunt Jenny would have been more than willing to ask her to help.

The third question was about my educational qualifications, or lack of them. Pupils leaving our junior secondary school were not given any kind of certificate and I was blissfully unaware that it was usual for applicants for nurse training to have Highers in Scotland; A levels in England. While the educational standards required for nursing were lower than for university and more academic professions, the main teaching hospitals such as the three large infirmaries in Glasgow insisted on Highers. However because the peripheral hospitals, like Hairmyres, had difficulties with recruitment they were willing to take students without formal qualifications. I explained I'd acquired the City and Guilds Certificate in Bricklaying and had successfully completed two thirds of the three-year course for the Ordinary National Certificate in Building Technology. These included maths, science and an adequate level of English . . . but she was unimpressed.

Despite all this I appeared to pass the interview and was sent to the School of Nursing to meet the senior sister tutor. She also interviewed me and then, to my surprise, said, 'Now we need to do an educational assessment.' Unaware that they set an entrance exam, I wasn't expecting this. She took me to a classroom and I was given what appeared to be an intelligence test and examinations in numeracy and literacy. At the end she went off with the papers but came back some time later to inform me that I'd passed.

Mary's Reaction

I went straight from hospital to Mary's home in time for her getting in from work. While she was pleased that I'd been successful and would be able to comply with the terms of my conditional registration as a conscientious objector, she had reservations. If I continued to work as a bricklayer we would be able to save up for a year or so and get married. Now our marriage would have to be put on hold for several years and what kind of income would I have even as a qualified nurse?

We took the bus to Blantyre to inform my parents. My father was out and Sadie, the prostitute who found solace with Mum, was visiting. Mum said, 'That's fine but do you think you'll manage all the studying?' I assured her I was confident of doing so.

Then Sadie turned to Mary and asked, 'What about you, hen? How do you feel about Jimmy spending so much time with all these lassies? What about the temptation?'

Mary didn't look too happy and replied, 'I don't like it but I trust him.' However, she wasn't very convincing.

Sadie then turned to Mum and said, 'Look Maggie, she's jealous.' I must confess I hadn't thought of this in my enthusiasm for my change of direction but I'm sure if the boot had been on the other foot I would have felt the same way.

Student Nurse

This was August 1958 and the next School of Nursing was due to start in a few weeks' time. I was given instructions about uniform and sent to a tailor in Glasgow to be fitted with a suit which was of a heavy, black serge material and very uncomfortable. We had to wear a white shirt and black tie and when on duty in the ward the jacket was to be removed and a white coat worn.

My first ward was Male Urology with Sister Thomson in charge. She was very strict and insisted on everything being done by the book. It was essential that patients drank lots and lots of water and my first job was to see that water carafes were regularly filled and patients constantly persuaded to drink, with intake and output being regularly recorded. On my first day I took a carafe from a locker, went to the kitchen and filled it, and then as I was walking up the ward I heard, 'Nurse, come back here.' I kept walking and the voice again said, 'Nurse, are you listening? Come back here.' Concentrating on the task in hand I continued on my way and was almost at the patient's bed when I felt a hand on my shoulder and turned to see Sister Thomson. She said, 'Nurse Graham, I am speaking to you. Did you not hear me?' The penny dropped I was the nurse and she was speaking to me.

'Sorry, Sister, I'm not used to be being called "nurse",' I replied. 'I'll pay attention in future.'

'Where is your tray?' she asked. 'You never carry things in your hand, always use a tray. Go back to the kitchen and get one.'

Although bricklaying was hard physical work, I found nursing to be at least as physical. In bricklaying we stood in the same position most of the time bending and straightening, lifting bricks, spreading mortar and laying the bricks. There was also heavy lifting of sills, lintels and steps. In nursing I rarely stood in the same position for more than a few minutes and must have walked for miles up and down the ward. There was just as much heavy lifting. Patients had to be rolled from side to side to change bed sheets, and had to be lifted up the bed to a comfortable sitting position without dragging them. A clean lift was required and this was done by two nurses without any lifting aids. Back problems are just as common among nurses as they are with builders.

Ward Hierarchy

I was familiar with the fairly simple hierarchy within the building industry, but getting to grips with hierarchy within nursing was more difficult.

Maids: At the lowest end were the maids, sometimes called domestics. Each ward had a maid who was occasionally assisted by a part-timer. The ward maid was responsible for cleaning the ward and side rooms. She could call on help from orderlies, auxiliary and junior student nurses to move patients' beds for cleaning. The kitchen was her kingdom and she ruled it with a rod of iron. She placed crockery and cutlery on a trolley and was assisted by junior nurses to lay them out on patients' bed tables or trays. Washing the dishes by hand was one of her duties. She did this using a thick slimy soapy mixture which was prepared the previous day by cutting washing soap into small pieces and placing them in a jar of water overnight.

Although she was considered the bottom of the heap, her role was vital and where the kitchen and cleanliness were concerned she would tear strips off anyone else, even the ward sister if necessary. I recall one occasion when a new and rather abrasive maid arrived in the ward. She strutted up and down the ward, walked into the duty room and told Sister the ward was filthy and she would not tolerate that. Sister was annoyed but simply said, 'I'm pleased you have high standards. Make sure you live up to them because I'll be watching you.'

Most maids had an important unofficial role with the patients. They were generally cheerful and chatted in a light-hearted way, cheering the patients up.

Orderlies and Auxiliary Nurses: Generally within our hospital, of the unqualified staff involved in direct patient care, men were orderlies and women were auxiliary nurses. The orderly had originated during the war when he assisted the nurses by doing some of the more menial tasks as well as the more intimate care of male patients, such as bathing and shaving pubic areas. Now they assisted the student and staff nurses with basic care such as bathing, bed-making and helping clean incontinent patients, and with serving meals. The orderlies were experts with open (cut-throat) razors when shaving, especially the pubic area of male patients, in preparation for surgery.

First and Second Year Student Nurses: We were next in the pecking order and while we started off with similar responsibilities to auxiliary nurses we gradually learned new skills partly in the classroom but mainly on the wards, being taught by more experienced students, the staff nurse and the sister/charge nurse.

State Enrolled Nurses (SENs): SENs were senior to the first and second year student nurses. Their roles too had originated during the war when young women with no nursing experience were enlisted to nurse wounded soldiers under the supervision of qualified nurses. Over the years of the war they acquired considerable knowledge and skill and this was recognised after the end of hostilities. They were given the status of State Enrolled Assistant Nurse (SEAN), later contracted to SEN. SENs had considerable responsibility within the ward but were restricted in some areas such as administering or supervising controlled drugs. The General Nursing Council recognised this grade and established a *roll*. They also established a two-year training course for the qualification which was suitable for young men and women who did not have the educational or intellectual qualifications for the three-year course leading to State Registration, especially in the larger city training hospitals.

Third Year Student Nurses: Since the SEN course was only two years, third-year students were given senior status to them. They were given more responsibilities especially in the administration of medicines and procedures such as passing naso-gastric tubes, catheterisation and supervising more junior students.

Staff Nurses: These were nurses who had successfully completed the three-year training course to gain registration with the General Nursing Council. They had the designation of State Registered Nurse (SRN) in England and Registered General Nurse (RGN) in Scotland.

Sister/Charge Nurse: The person in charge of the ward or department was Sister if female or Charge Nurse if male. She or he had overall responsibility for the running of the ward, including responsibility for patient care, staff and ward administration. Most had several years' experience post-registration. They usually had at least one other nursing qualification, midwifery and psychiatric nursing being common.

Typical Day

The typical day in hospital went as follows: arrive at 8 am and help the night staff to clear up the breakfast dishes. All beds were then pulled out into the middle of the ward by student and auxiliary nurses to allow the domestics to vacuum and wash the floors beneath the beds, and dust and wash all ledges behind them. After putting the beds back in place there was a bedpan and urine bottle round, then a bed-making round. Patients who were fit to get out of bed were allowed to sit up. Beds were stripped and bedclothes changed.

For patients who were not allowed out of bed the bottom sheets were changed by rolling the patient from side to side, and their pressure areas rubbed to prevent bedsores. This involved rubbing the buttocks, heels, elbows and shoulders vigorously with soapy water, drying and then rubbing them with methylated spirit. The theory was that vigorous rubbing stimulated the circulation and methylated spirit helped toughen the skin, making it less likely to break down. Incontinent patients were cleaned with tow, which is a bundle of the coarse and broken part of flax or hemp. It looked like horse hair but much coarser. We were still enduring post-war austerity and kinder materials were not readily accessible. In later years unbleached cotton wool became available.

Then all patients had to get back into bed for the ward rounds. Although we did our best to make patients as comfortable as possible, this was more of a military-style drill. All bedclothes were neatly tucked in with boxed corners and the patients looking like trussed chickens. The first round was by senior nursing staff such as Matron or one of her deputies. Beds had to be in a straight line to the inch, white top sheets were folded over the counterpane to a regulation distance of 12 inches and a red blanket was folded over the foot of the bed to a regulation width of 18 inches. Sister or Staff Nurse took her round and gave a brief report on each patient. Any discrepancy in the neat line of beds and bedclothes would be pointed out.

There followed the consultant's round with treatments discussed and anyone ready for home discharged. There wasn't a sound during this time. I was recently a patient in a Glasgow hospital and was amazed at the difference during ward rounds now. The consultant physician did her ward round with ambulant patients walking about and chatting to other patients. Tea ladies did their rounds and the shop trolley came, and then two workmen arrived to repair broken ceiling tiles and did some hammering. The contrast with the silent 1950s was stark.

On reflection the consultant physician demanded hush back then because he or she needed complete silence to hear subtle differences in lung or heart sounds which were vital in arriving at an accurate diagnosis—not to mention that they were treated like gods, and expected to be. Today physicians are much more reliant on technology and vital old skills may have been lost or at least diminished.

Afterwards patients had a cup of tea and staff too had a tea break, then there was a dressings and medicines round and it was time for bed baths and more work on pressure points. Trays and tables were prepared for lunch and when the food arrived it was plated by the sister or nurse in charge, and all grades of nurses served and helped those who needed help. Sister kept a watchful eye on proceedings to make sure no one was neglected. They were of course the old Nightingale, open style of wards with twelve to fourteen patients on each side.

After lunch there was another bedpan and bottle round then bed-making and pressure-point round. Basins were taken to bed-bound patients and those who were ambulant went to the washroom, and it was everyone back to bed to be neatly packaged again, this time for the visitors.

During visiting hour we couldn't do the usual patient care, other than anything urgent, so we did other chores. All dressings and appliances were prepared in the ward. Nothing was disposable. Glass syringes were wrapped in gauze and sterilised in a boiler. Needles were checked and if they looked blunt they were sent to be sharpened but they were never really sharp compared with modern needles. Those deemed sharp enough were boiled with the syringes. Dressings were of folded gauze and we made the swabs. Wounds were cleaned with cotton wool balls and we made them up from a large roll of cotton wool. These dressing materials were packed in drums ready to be sent to the central autoclave to be sterilised.

Another visiting hour chore was urine-testing in the sluice room. This was before the advent of dipstick tests and urine was tested with a variety of chemical reagents and by heating. Bedpans and urine bottles were metal or hard plastic and had to be sterilised in the sluice.

After visiting there was another cup of tea then yet another bed-making and pressure area round. There would be another medicine round and all patients had their TPR checked; that is temperature, pulse and respiration.

In surgical wards patients came in two days before the operation to be prepared for surgery. A strong laxative was given two nights before and then on the day before surgery an *enema saponis*, soap and water enema, was given. This was prepared by making a solution with soft green soap and warm water and between half a pint and a pint of this was poured into the patient's large bowel through a funnel and tube. The procedure was usually carried out at the patient's bed and then he or she was asked to wait as long as possible before going to the toilet. The ideal was thirty minutes but this was rarely achieved and there were occasional 'accidents' en route.

Another preoperative preparation was shaving. Anyone for abdominal or urological surgery had all hair on the trunk and pubic area shaved off and the area disinfected with an antiseptic liquid, often chlorhexidine. There were orderlies who helped with the shaving and some of them were very proficient with the old cut-throat type of razor. As a student nurse who had only ever used an electric razor to shave my face I didn't dare go near those delicate areas with an open razor in case I performed my own unintended surgery. I used a safety razor.

On theatre days patients had to be made ready. No food or fluid was allowed and about thirty minutes before being taken to theatre they were given an injection to sedate them and dry up the mouth and stomach to prevent vomiting during the operation. Patients returning from theatre required more concentrated observation including care of drainage tubes and intra-venous drips.

This sort of routine continued through the evening. What is clear from the above is that the day was punctuated by regular rounds so every patient was visited and checked regularly. In addition there were four medicine rounds per day around the three main meal times and just before lights out. Student nurses were supervised at first but were allowed to do the medicine round unsupervised from the second year on.

Sometimes elderly patients could be resistant to taking their medication and we were taught to be creative in trying to persuade them. I remember Mr Elder, who was always reluctant to take his antibiotic capsules and often stubbornly refused. He liked jam so I opened the capsule and mixed the antibiotic powder with some jam on a spoon. This was accepted but only for two seconds. As soon as he tasted the antibiotic he spat it out with great force all over me. Lesson learned! Antibiotics taste foul which is why they're put in capsules.

In preparation for our ward's receiving days, that is days when it was our ward's turn to receive emergencies, as many patients as possible were discharged the day before to make beds available. On the receiving day patients were admitted to the empty beds and if demand exceeded the availability of beds, more were brought in. First of all, the beds were pushed closer together to accommodate two extra beds on each side of the ward and if that still wasn't enough two or three beds were put in the middle of the ward. Telephone calls were made round the wards to find empty beds to send some of those due for discharge in a few days' time.

Income Supplement

When I received my first nursing salary I realised just how much my income had dropped from that of a final-year apprentice bricklayer to that of a first-year student nurse. Would I manage and would my mother manage? I had an arrangement as an apprentice where I handed her half my basic wage and a quarter of my bonus. I realised my monthly salary was now less than a week's wages previously, so how could I supplement my income? I was a bit of a sucker for slick advertising and saw an advert for a *garden scythe*. This was like a 12 inch-long safety razor on a broom handle and was advertised as being faster and neater than a lawn mower. The very thing, I thought. It seemed that many people in their new council houses were struggling to keep their front lawns neat and tidy so I could do the job for them when not on duty. I sent for the implement and set about using it. Uncle Tam and Aunt Agnes agreed to let me use it on their lawn to test it. It was a disaster. It took three or four times longer than a lawn mower and chewed up the lawn. That was the end of that.

The next scheme was again a response to a slick advertisement. This company was looking for people to make shopping bags with a synthetic leather material. The deal was, I bought the material from them, made the bags and then sold them back to them, or I could sell some privately if I wanted. Great, I thought, I can do this. We didn't have a sewing machine but undaunted I invested in one, buying it on hire purchase. Then I purchased my first batch of material with which I received the pattern for the bags. I made my first few bags with little difficulty but it was time-consuming.

Aunt Jenny and Mum bought my first two bags and I sent off the next two to the company for approval. They were returned with a note telling me where they needed improvement. I made the necessary corrections and sent off the next batch only to receive another rejection. After another couple of rejections it dawned on me. I had been conned. They were only interested in selling to me and had no intention of buying from me.

The solution to my dilemma came soon after that when two elderly sisters who lived together in an old tenement asked me if I'd be willing or able to repair and point a brick outhouse for them. I said, 'Yes, as long as I can do it at times to suit my off duty.' I did that and earned some extra money, and this led to my being asked to do occasional small building jobs by other people. Why hadn't I thought of that before? I was still a fully qualified bricklayer.

Formal Teaching

The first three months of formal teaching were in the classroom except for Sundays when we worked in the wards. During these three months of Preliminary Training School (PTS) we were taught anatomy, physiology, hygiene, community health, some basic nursing procedures and cookery for invalids. Some of the foods we were taught to prepare included: beef tea, poached fish, cheese soufflé, junket, fruit and vegetable juice as well as boiled, poached and scrambled eggs. This was followed by an examination. It was part written and part practical including a cookery exam. I was asked to cook a cheese soufflé and recall that I forgot to add salt. Fortunately the cheese provided enough flavour and the examiner didn't notice.

I learned in PTS that it's not a good idea to contradict your senior, especially the tutor. During the community health lectures the tutor was extolling the health benefits of the new Clean Air Act which had recently come into force. She told us how smoke goes into the air causing pollution and fog. Then she set about explaining what occurs in a domestic fire. She said, 'As the coal burns it takes oxygen out of the air in the room and replaces it with carbon dioxide.'

We were allowed to interrupt to ask questions so using my building knowledge I said, 'Excuse me; that's wrong. When the coal burns it doesn't take oxygen out of the air in the room. The air with the depleted oxygen and increased carbon dioxide goes up the chimney. New fresh air comes into the room to replace it.'

She glowered at me for a moment and then said, 'It doesn't alter the fact that coal fires produce pollution. Just think of the benefit we'll all get from clean air.' Later she told me, 'Ask questions but don't contradict me in front of others. If you feel the need to challenge something, do it in private.' I apologised and she graciously accepted.

There were about twelve students in our class, of which five were male. Two of the male students had been orderlies who had decided to do the training. They were both married and received a supplement to their student salary, but after two months they gave up. The student salary, even with the supplement, just wasn't enough to live on.

We had a Saturday off while in PTS and always worked on Sunday, alternating mornings with afternoon and evenings. Sundays were always arranged like that even when we were full-time in the wards. I had always refused to work on Sundays when in the building industry but now there was no choice; sick people had to be nursed, and this was completely consistent with Jesus' teaching and actions on the Sabbath.

Urology Ward

The period of time we were assigned to a particular ward, department or the classroom was referred to as a *block*. My first ward block was back in Urology with Sister Thomson and I returned there several times during my training. On one occasion during visiting hour when I was sterilising syringes and needles, one of the syringes broke and Sister Thomson was annoyed at me for allowing this to happen. The wards were heated by a low pressure hot water system with two large six-inch pipes running just above the floor along the length of the ward. Sister Thomson was quite small, about 5ft 2in., and I was 6ft 1in. tall so she stood on the heating pipes to get up to my level and told me off, wagging her finger, telling me how expensive equipment was and how I must learn to be more careful.

Most of the ward teaching was about nursing procedures, usually on the basis of being shown it, then doing one supervised, and then if satisfactory being allowed to get on with it. 'See it, do it, teach it,' was the saying, and we learned a lot from more senior students.

Male nurses were not allowed to nurse female patients, full stop, and female student nurses were not allowed to catheterise male patients. This involved passing a catheter along the urethra which runs a slightly tortuous course through the penis then through the prostate gland and into the bladder. It was carried out to empty the bladders of patients who were unable to do so naturally (very painful), or to keep the urine flowing after surgery. Male students were taught this procedure early in training although we weren't allowed to do it for the first time on any patient. It had to be done by a doctor.

One day when I was in my second year we had a patient who had been catheterised for an acute retention of urine and it was decided to remove his catheter to see if he could pass water naturally. We were giving him lots of fluid to drink, just as we should, and Sister Thomson went off for her tea break leaving a third-year female student in charge. Very soon the patient's bladder filled and he was unable to urinate. This quickly became painful and I said I would catheterise him. My senior said, 'No, we must wait till Sister gets back.' However he was getting very uncomfortable and I said, 'I must do this,' but she refused to allow me and the patient became increasingly distressed.

When Sister returned I was sent straight away to insert the catheter, with immediate relief for the patient. Sister called the third-year student to the office and gave her a telling off and then I was called. I was a little surprised because I didn't think I had done anything wrong. She told me I shouldn't have allowed a patient to suffer in that way, so I said, 'I'm only second year and I have to obey my seniors.'

Sister Thomson replied, 'You have a duty to relieve pain and if you have the means to do so, you must do it and take the consequences, no matter who refuses to give you permission.' These are words I have never forgotten.

Patients died from time to time and learning the 'last offices' was an important part of our training. I remember very clearly the first time I was taken to carry out the last offices. Just a few weeks after starting as a student nurse a staff nurse took me behind a screen where there was a dead body. Among the other procedures we carried out was washing the man down with Dettol, pushing cotton wool into all orifices to prevent leakage of bodily fluids, and tying the feet and ankles together and the hands to the side of the body to facilitate lifting and carrying. To this day the smell of Dettol reminds me of death.

At mealtimes the tea was made in the ward kitchen, and simple meals such as boiled, poached or scrambled eggs were cooked in the kitchen for patients who preferred that to the hospital meal on offer, so long as they supplied the eggs. Sister Thomson was very strict and taught me a lot of skills which have been very useful to me throughout my career, and I've always had great admiration for her. She was never moody except once. I was in the kitchen getting the evening meal ready for serving, and had made the tea in the large teapot. She stormed in, face like thunder and said, 'Nurse, did you heat that teapot before making the tea?'

'Yes, Sister; I always do.'

'What did you heat it with?' she asked.

I pointed to the kettle. 'Water from there.' Without further comment she turned on her heels and walked out, leaving me very puzzled. I never discovered why she'd been so cross.

There was one area, however, which escaped her strict discipline. She delegated the ordering of supplies for the ward, including drugs, to her staff nurse. When the drugs arrived they were checked and put away either by the staff nurse on duty in the evening or by the night duty staff nurse.

I came in one morning on Sister Thomson's day off to overhear a furious row in the duty room between the day staff nurse, Nurse McLean, who had just come on and the male night staff nurse, Nurse Stewart, who was about to go off duty. Nurse McLean had ordered a substantial supply of Drinamyl but Nurse Stewart had removed almost all of it and taken it for himself. She was furious about this because they had an agreement that they would share the spoils. Drinamyl tablets, otherwise known as purple hearts, contained a stimulant; dexamphetamine and a sedative; amylobarbitone, intended for use as an antidepressant. It was widely abused by young people at parties. Amphetamines and barbiturates were also abused to some extent by staff in hospital, especially married women on night duty. They took the amphetamine to stimulate them at work, and then took a barbiturate sleeping tablet on going to bed in the morning. Although drugs which came under the control of the Dangerous Drugs Act, such as morphine and heroin, were strictly controlled with a drugs register, there appeared to be little or no control of amphetamines and barbiturates.

Surgical Ward

After my first spell in Urology I was moved next door to Male Surgical with Sister Muir who was very different from Sister Thomson; not so strict and more relaxed about doing everything by the book. She was pretty and petite but spent very little time in the ward apart from doing the ward rounds and wound dressings. The rest of her time was mostly spent doing essential administrative work—and she spent a lot of time in her office flirting with junior doctors. She was usually pleasant, except at certain times of the month. At those junctures there was a lot of shouting at junior staff with things being thrown halfway up the ward in fits of temper.

Occasionally if a patient needed close supervision, one nurse would be assigned to that patient only. This was referred to as *specialing*. During my first period in the surgical ward I was asked to *special* a new admission one evening. He was drunk and had been admitted unconscious with a severe head injury. My job for the next four hours was to observe his level of consciousness and check his pulse and blood pressure every fifteen minutes.

I checked for response to speech and painful stimuli such as pricking his ears but there was no response at first. Two hours or so later he began to respond to painful stimuli but nothing else. His pulse remained steady as did his blood pressure. At that time nurses did not use stethoscopes. They were the badge of office of doctors. We felt the pulse at the wrist and blew up the blood pressure cuff till we could no longer feel the pulse and then noted the level it reappeared again as we deflated the cuff. This gave the systolic pressure.

At the end of my four-hour stint I had to write a report to give to Sister before going off duty. I was still teetotal at this time and had a judgemental attitude to alcohol, especially excess. My report began, 'This man had been drinking alcohol to excess and in his drunken state he fell down stairs and sustained a serious head injury. He was admitted unconscious but it is not clear how much of this is due to alcohol abuse and how much is due to the head injury. He remains unconscious but there is some evidence of recovery in that he now responds to painful stimuli but not to speech or loud sounds. His pulse and blood pressure remain stable as shown by the chart.'

My report and the chart were on a clipboard and I handed them to Sister who read my report. She glared at me for a second and then threw them straight at me but I managed to duck just in time to avoid my own head injury. She said, 'It's not your place to judge patients. It's your duty to care for them in a non-judgemental manner. Go away and rewrite your report. Give your patient his name; Mr Bell. You may not use terms such as "drunken state" but it is acceptable to say that he appeared to be under the influence of alcohol or a drug.' A valuable lesson was learned.

Another patient I nursed in this ward comes to mind, Mr Anderson, who was admitted for gall bladder surgery. Things didn't go well after the operation and he was leaking bile from his wound. He was on intravenous fluids because he was unable to take adequate food and fluids by mouth. Despite all efforts his blood pressure was dropping, he looked increasingly toxic and was becoming rather confused.

I was sent to change his intravenous drip bottle and as I leant over, he grabbed my scissors from my top pocket and stabbed me in the arm. Before I could compose myself, he took a swing at me, landing a blow on my chin. No serious harm was done since he was quite feeble. A superficial stab wound on my arm and a small bruise on my chin were the only visible effects but I was a little shaken. He was sedated and transferred to the specialist Liver Unit at Glasgow Royal Infirmary.

Over the next two weeks I was having scheduled dental treatment, as a result of which I had two front teeth extracted in preparation for a part-denture. A few days after the extractions, but before my part-denture was ready, I went on duty to find Mr Anderson back in the ward, looking well and sitting up in bed. He called me over, smiled sheepishly and said, 'I understand I assaulted you. Please accept my apologies. I don't remember any of it.'

I smiled and accepted his apology, saying, 'It wasn't your fault. You were ill and didn't know what you were doing.'

His face froze suddenly as he saw my toothless smile and said, 'Did I do that to you?'

I reassured him.

Mr Philips was another memorable patient. He was a very pleasant elderly man who was admitted for abdominal surgery. Being very ill at the time, he was in the first bed. During visiting hour one day I was making swabs and packing drums for sterilisation next to his bed. I chatted a bit with his daughter and pointed out that I knew her father from several years earlier. He was the same Mr Philips who ran the small shop in Stoney-meadow. I recalled our cycling trips and the fact that we always bought Wagon Wheels. She said how pleased she was and promised to bring me a box of the biscuits from the shop.

Fortunately the surgery was successful and I was able to have occasional conversations with him and reminisce about our cycling trips to his shop. He was later discharged and when they were leaving the ward his daughter left a box of Wagon Wheels with Sister who proceeded to distribute them among the staff including me. At first I was rather miffed, thinking, this box of Wagon Wheels was meant for me, not for everyone. I was just about to say so but drew myself up, thinking, how selfish can you be?

Medical Ward

Sister McLean, a married, middle-aged lady, was in charge of the male medical ward. This was unusual since most of the sisters were single, and left when they married. She was strict yet fair and did her best to maintain a happy atmosphere in her ward.

Patients in medical wards were generally older and with more life-threatening illnesses than in the surgical wards. Acute exacerbations of chronic lung conditions, heart attacks and heart failure made up a large proportion of patients in the ward at a given time. The death rate was much higher in medical wards than in surgical. Going on duty in the morning, it was usually possible to tell if there'd been a death during the night because a gloom had descended on the ward.

On one occasion I returned from my tea break and walked into the ward to see Mr Watson sitting up in bed looking calm and happy. He had been admitted with a heart attack the previous day and was still having chest pain despite the regular medication. He was anxious and fairly agitated most of the time so it was a surprise to see him looking so relaxed.

As I walked towards him to say I was pleased to see him looking better, I realised there was no response to my approach. He was just staring ahead and when I got right up to him I found he wasn't breathing. This was my second experience of a cardiac arrest. You may recall my first was when my uncle Tom died suddenly in 1948. I screened Mr Watson off and informed Sister who called the doctor to officially confirm death. This was before cardiopulmonary resuscitation (CPR), and well before the value of aspirin in reducing death from heart attacks was recognised.

One other memorable event occurred during my second period in the medical ward when I was in my third year. It didn't seem like very much at the time. Sister McLean asked me to go to the drug cupboard and medicine trolley to remove all Distaval tablets.

She said, 'You must check very carefully that they're all removed. Bring them to me and I'll send them back to the pharmacy to be destroyed.'

On taking them to her, I asked, 'What's wrong with Distaval?' It was thought to be one of the safest drugs we had available and couldn't cause death even in large overdose.

She said, 'What do we use it for?'

I replied, 'It's a very useful and safe sedative. It's helpful in the treatment of asthma and is used for pregnancy sickness, though obviously not on this ward.'

She smiled, then looked serious and said, 'That's what we thought, but we've been informed that it causes serious defects in unborn babies. Many die before they're born and those who survive have serious defects of the limbs and internal organs.'

We were expected to know the generic name of the drugs we used as well as their trade names, and she said, 'What's the generic name of Distaval?'

I had to think for a moment and then replied, 'Thalidomide.'

'That's right,' she said. 'Remember these names, because it's been sold without prescription in some countries and been used widely here. Many people may have it in their cupboards at home.' Sadly this was to affect many people's lives for years to come.

Ignorant Assumption

During a period on night duty in the medical ward I had a patient, Mr Ingles. He had been admitted with breathlessness but had improved to some extent. When I came on duty in the evening he appeared bright with no evidence of breathlessness but around 3 or 4 am he became breathless. I telephoned the doctor who came to see him and ordered an intramuscular injection which I gave him. This appeared to relieve the breathlessness and he settled and went back to sleep after half an hour or so.

The following night the same thing happened and when I called the duty doctor he simply authorized the injection by telephone. As before, Mr Ingles settled and went back to sleep. This routine continued and by the fourth night I had decided that my patient was suffering from anxiety and the injection was simply acting as a placebo. Feeling guilty at disturbing the doctor every night for this I took it upon myself to give Mr Ingles an injection of sterile water. This time there was no improvement and he called me again to say he was no better. Realizing I had been presumptuous and had made a mistake, I telephoned for authorisation for the proper drug and the patient settled as before.

When I gave Sister the report in the morning, I had to confess to my misdemeanour. As I said previously, Sister Mclean was stern but fair. She looked annoyed and said, 'I hope you've learned a lesson. We are nurses and our duty is to carry out the instructions of the doctor. If you want to make this kind of clinical decision, you need to train to be a doctor, not a nurse.' She explained that Mr Ingles had paroxysmal nocturnal dyspnoea (PND), a condition associated with heart failure and lung conditions. 'Read up on it and I'll ask you about it when you come on duty after your nights off. If you show me you understand the condition we'll say no more about it.'

An important lesson was learned, but her comment about needing to study as a doctor to be able to make that sort of clinical decision gave me food for thought.

Self-Promotion

With reference to ward hierarchy, we had an SEN in the medical ward who strutted up and down the ward in a way the sister never did. She was an unmarried lady who was nearing retirement age and liked to be referred to as Miss Sloan. Because she'd been a nurse during the war she was one of the original assistant nurses who was later entered in the roll. She'd been on this ward for many years so she knew the routine like the back of her hand. At visiting times she decided when the doors would be opened and when the bell would be rung to signal the end of visiting. Many visitors thought she was the sister and addressed her as such. She never corrected them and indeed she acted like Sister with the students, refusing to acknowledge that third-year students were her senior.

I spent three periods in this ward, once in first year, once on night duty in second year and once in third year. During my first year Nurse Sloan was very helpful and taught me much about nursing medical conditions. I had no real contact with her during my spell on night duty but when I returned early in my third year and therefore senior to her she pretended I was junior and refused to take instructions from me. SENs and third-year students were often left in charge of the ward during the evening but always with a qualified staff nurse or sister available in an adjacent ward. When we were on together I was in charge and it was difficult to make her accept this. However we came to a compromise; she could make decisions regarding opening doors for visitors and serving meals but I would make the clinical decisions and she had to accept them.

Unfortunately her vision was deteriorating and she was making mistakes with medication and other matters requiring reading or good near vision. At first she refused to admit to a problem but Sister insisted she have a senior student supervise her. This was often my duty but it became too much for her to take and she took early retirement, much to everyone's relief.

Later in my third year I was attached to a district nurse for a week to learn something of their work. She was Sister Green and before going to the patients' homes she told me a little about them and why we were visiting. Before one visit she said, 'This lady's blind and needs daily eye drops. She's a retired deputy matron and tends to ask awkward questions to try and catch us out. You can give her the eye drops.'

When we entered she said, 'Hello Miss Sloan, I've brought a student nurse today. This is Nurse Graham. Do you mind if he puts your drops in?'

'Has he done this before?'

At this I moved forward and took her hand and shook it. I replied, 'Yes, many times and I'll be very grateful if you'll allow me to put your eye drops in.' I had recognised her as our SEN from the medical ward as soon as I saw her and when I spoke I'm sure she recognised my voice but neither of us acknowledged this.

She said, 'Yes, that's fine.'

After I'd completed the procedure and we were about to leave, the patient said to Sister Green in that pompous tone I was so familiar with, 'I'd like to speak to your student alone. I want to ask him a few questions.'

Sister, expecting me to get a grilling on my knowledge replied, 'I don't think it's your duty to test my student's knowledge.' Having an idea of what she wanted to say, I reassured Sister that I was happy for her to ask me some questions on my own so she went out to her car.

Miss Sloan said, 'I recognise your voice. You're Jimmy Graham aren't you?'

'I am and it's lovely to meet you again,' I replied.

'I'm delighted to meet you again,' she responded, 'but I have a concern. They all think I'm a retired deputy matron. I suppose this will be me demoted now.'

'No, you served your country well both during the war and for a great many years in the NHS, and you taught me a lot as a junior. It's our secret.'

When I returned to the car Sister said, 'I hope she didn't give you a hard time.'

'No,' I replied, 'she just asked a few basic questions, nothing I couldn't handle.

Road Accident

Very early in our PTS training we witnessed a serious road accident when on the bus on the way to hospital one morning. There was a collision between two cars and one man was seriously injured. Nurses were available to give immediate assistance and an ambulance was called. After the casualty was loaded into the ambulance it sped off up the road towards the hospital, but after only 300 yards it too was involved in a head-on collision. We were shocked and all felt very sorry for the poor man who had now been involved in two major accidents, but he wasn't the only casualty this time and the most serious was Jack, the ambulance driver. He was unconscious so another ambulance was called and took both casualties to hospital.

The man who had been injured in the first accident had broken limbs and was admitted for surgery and immobilisation but was discharged a few weeks later. He eventually made a full recovery. Jack on the other hand remained unconscious for many months. I helped to nurse him during my block with Sister Muir in Ward 21. Because he was unconscious he was fed through a gastric tube so was always bypassed at meal times. Sadly Jack eventually died.

Wrong Diagnosis

Take a step back to our Preliminary Training School. After the three-month course we had the examination the following Monday, but on the Sunday morning as I was dressing to go on duty I had a sudden, severe pain in my left testicle like a hard kick. It quickly swelled and I felt sick and faint. Not sure how to describe the problem to my parents I simply said, 'I'm not well and need a doctor.' Without asking any questions they sent for the doctor.

He arrived an hour or so later and examined me then said, 'You have epididymitis which is an infection behind your testicle. I'll prescribe an antibiotic and a scrotal support to relieve the discomfort.' He wrote the prescription and a medical certificate to let me stay off work for two weeks and left. I assume he explained the problem to my parents since they didn't ask me what was wrong.

When I didn't turn up for the PTS examination the tutor assumed I'd got cold feet. However the medical certificate corrected that. I gradually improved over the two weeks and went back to work. I still had the examination to sit but Miss Sclater, the senior tutor, said I could sit it with the next intake four months later.

All went well for two months or so and then I developed an abscess in the same area. This was during my time in Ward 21 and I was prescribed penicillin injections daily for a week. In order to avoid my having to take time off work it was decided I should have the injections at work, so each day when I reported for duty I went into Sister Muir's office and dropped my trousers to get what felt like a good kick in the buttock.

The problem didn't resolve itself and I was referred to the surgical clinic where I was examined by Mr Macrossan, the senior consultant, who did tests and then informed me my GP had made a mistake. I had not had epididymitis but a torsion of the left testicle. This is where the testicle twists and cuts off the blood supply, causing tissue death (necrosis). Instead of prescribing antibiotics my GP should have had me admitted as an emergency to correct the twist and restore the blood supply. Now the only remedy would be surgery to remove the necrotic testicle.

I was admitted one day after Jack died. Being staff I was put in the first bed with a screen round me, exactly as Jack had been. After so many months of ignoring this bed at mealtimes the staff continued to do so and I had to keep popping my head through the screen to say, 'Excuse me, I'm here now.'

Concerned relatives always want to know what's wrong and ours were no exception. Mary's mum asked her what was wrong with me, and since they'd never discussed anything intimate, Mary was unsure how to answer.

She simply said, 'You know these things men have? Well, he's having it cut off.'

Her mother looked shocked and said, 'That's serious. If you continue this relationship you'll never have any children. It's a big sacrifice.' I can only imagine what the poor woman thought was being cut off. Fortunately we can function completely on all levels with one healthy testicle just as one healthy kidney provides normal renal function. I made a good and speedy recovery and was soon back on duty.

Sunday Difficulties

The Sunday duty rota created difficulties for me with church attendance. The Sunday morning service, affectionately known as 'the morning meeting', was always a Communion service and considered the most important service of the week, but it finished around 12.30 pm, too late for me to walk to High Blantyre to get a bus to Hairmyres Hospital. I tried leaving early but that disturbed the service, so I stopped going for a while. I was still able to attend the evening service once a fortnight in theory but my arrangement with Mary was that we alternated my free Sunday evenings between her church in Cambuslang and mine in Blantyre. The result was my attendance at Bethany Hall, Blantyre was about once a month in the evening but nil in the all-important Sunday mornings.

Step in the Scotts again! No doubt there was some family discussion unknown to me and I was approached by George Young, the husband of Isabel, the theatre sister in Hairmyres and niece of Aunt Jenny and Uncle George Scott. He had a car and offered to give me a lift on the alternate Sunday mornings I was able to attend. That worked for a while but he wasn't in the habit of going to church very often and it meant that either he had to come to the service every two weeks or turn up at the end and wait for me coming out. This seemed to me to be a bit of an imposition and I felt increasingly uncomfortable so another solution had to be found.

My Scooter

Mary had a friend whose boyfriend owned a motorcycle, and they were enjoying going all over the country on it,

Image 7-1: On my scooter at
Cowan Wilson Avenue

so she suggested I get one. It was a time of mods and rockers, and scooters were very much in fashion. Scooters appealed to me more than motorcycles, so I decided to get one. I discovered one I liked, a Diana Durkopp, and ordered one. It had a 200cc two-stroke engine and was more powerful than the more common Vespa and Lambretta scooters at the time. When it was ready for me to collect, I went along armed with my L plates and provisional licence, never having been on one let alone driven one, but I was quite confident because I'd cycled all over Scotland and knew the Highway Code.

The salesman very helpfully took me out to a piece of waste ground behind the showroom and showed me the controls. He let me sit on the pillion while he drove to demonstrate.

Then he said, 'Now you take the controls and I'll sit behind you.' I stalled a couple of times and he said, 'Give it more gas and let out the clutch a little more slowly.' I gave it so much throttle that I shot off and the salesman fell off the back. That was enough; there was a limit to his helpfulness, so he left me to practise on my own before taking it on to the road. Needless to say, my competence on the road was abysmal but I did get home safely.

That did the job and I was able to go to church and still get to work on time. It all started well and travel to the hospital was much easier on Sundays and all other days, but I soon ran into trouble. The engine of my scooter was air-cooled and the nut holding the fan kept working loose, causing the engine to overheat. It cut out a few times resulting in my being late. After two or three occasions I was summoned to Matron's office and told in no uncertain terms that I must get a reliable form of transport. I took it back to the garage and they fixed it, making my timekeeping impeccable from then on.

A Lovely Girlfriend

Isabel Young, Uncle George's niece, was Sister in the general theatre so I never had any direct professional contact with her. However, apart from her husband's help with my Sunday transport, there were three occasions when our paths crossed indirectly.

Not all of a nurse's time in theatre is spent at operations. The theatre has to be prepared with trays laid out with the relevant sterile instruments, swabs and drapes for the proposed operations. Oxygen and anaesthetic cylinders have to be checked with spares available. Following the operations, instruments were cleaned and gloves cleaned and checked for punctures. Any punctures were repaired during post-war austerity and all were sent off to be sterilised. During these more relaxed procedures there was time for girly talk among the student nurses and Sister often joined in. Male student nurses were not allowed in the general theatre.

Being outnumbered four or five to one in the hospital, unattached male nurses had the pick of the crop with the girls. Some formed stable relationships early on while some did the rounds with a few gaining a reputation for sleeping around. One I recall very clearly, Andrew Evans, was a first-year student nurse. He had wanted to be a doctor but didn't get the grades he needed so decided on nursing instead. He frequently boasted of his conquests and was caught in bed with a female student one afternoon when the home sister did an unexpected inspection of the student nurses' quarters. He and the girl were called before Matron and given a stern reprimand but no further action was taken. His ward reports from the sisters were not satisfactory and when two months later he was caught again with a different girl he was dismissed instantly. Matron's comment was, 'You will never be a nurse. Sweeping streets is all you're good for.' An insult to street sweepers, I think!

I was thought to be quite handsome and having come from bricklaying I had lost my childhood fat and replaced it with muscle. During one of these girly chats in theatre one of the students was saying she fancied me and wondered how best to attract my attention. Sister Young heard her and said, 'Forget it. You've no chance with him. He already has a lovely girlfriend.'

On another occasion I was being discussed by a different group. This time they were wondering why I didn't play the field and one suggested that I probably had no interest in girls. Although homosexual sex was still illegal at this time it was recognised that two or possibly three of the male nurses were gay. This was discussed in whispers but again Sister Young was close enough to hear them. She quickly put them straight saying, 'You're way off beam on that one. He does like girls. He has a lovely girlfriend.'

On the third occasion I did meet her briefly to get a telling off. Earlier that day while I was in Urology near the time to go off duty, Sister Thomson asked me to catheterise Mr McManus and take a first-year student, Nurse Robinson, to show her how it's done. Although she wouldn't be expected to catheterise males she needed to know how to set up a trolley in preparation for a doctor carrying out the procedure. I laid out the trolley with a sterile cover and then the catheter, lubricant, swabs, forceps, syringe, sterile water and so on. All was well and she appeared interested.

During the procedure I reached the stage where, after cleaning the penis, I picked it up with a sterile swab, injected lubricant into the urethra and then, taking the catheter in forceps, I inserted it into the urethra. Suddenly and without warning she fainted and landed in a heap on the floor. Unsure whether to leave my patient and attend to my student or leave the student and continue the procedure I called for help. An auxiliary nurse arrived quickly just as Nurse Robinson was coming round so I continued to see to my patient. After cleaning up we were off duty and I left the building to get my scooter, which was parked near the theatre window. The first-year student was just a few yards in front of me and was clearly still rather wobbly after her faint. Trying to be light-hearted I called after her, 'Nurse Robinson, would you like a run on my scooter?'

I expected her to smile and say, 'No way,' or words to that effect. Instead she turned and said, 'Oh, yes please.' I couldn't get out of it so I helped her on to the pillion and took her for a short run around the hospital grounds.

After returning to the same spot I helped her off and was about to go home when I heard a voice from the open theatre window, 'Nurse Graham, come in here at

Image 7-2: Mary, my lovely girlfriend

once.' Once inside I was confronted by my relative who said, 'What do you think you're doing flirting with that girl, Jimmy Graham? You have a lovely girlfriend.' I tried to explain the background and that it was a clumsy attempt at a joke gone wrong.

Unsure whether or not she believed me, I continued, 'If you don't believe me, ask Sister Thomson. She knows what happened.' I think she did believe me because she knew from listening to her students that I was a bit of an enigma, leaving them unsure of my sexual orientation.

Driving Test

Having the scooter not only made travelling to work easier but greatly improved my leisure time. Mary was keen to get on it, but wasn't allowed so long as I only had a provisional licence, so I arranged my driving test for about two months after getting the scooter. We arranged to go to Aunt Jean's at Wanlockhead for a week right after the test. The possibility of failing the test didn't occur to us. After all, I'd cycled on main roads all over Scotland. But I did fail, and since we had the holiday arranged we had to quickly form Plan B.

This strict law-abiding chap, who had walked home from Larkhall in the middle of the night rather than cycle without a front lamp, now decided to bend the rules. I took my L plates off and Mary came with me as a pillion passenger for the week's holiday. We enjoyed the holiday and having the freedom to explore the Southern Uplands was wonderful, but we were always aware that we could get in trouble.

On one occasion we stopped at a filling station in the village of Crawford on the main A74 road south to get petrol. Just as I was paying, a policeman walked in and we left hurriedly. As we rode out on to the A74 I thought

I heard someone calling after me but kept going only to find we were being pursued by a motorcycle. He caught up with us and stopped us. We were so relieved to find it wasn't the policeman but the filling station attendant standing with five shillings in his hand.

'You forgot your change,' he said.

Spills

With its small wheels the scooter tended to be top heavy and it was common, on wet or slippery roads, for the wheels to slide to the side tipping me on to the tarmac. I soon learned techniques to avoid this most of the time. There was one occasion when going south on the A74, the main route to London, I was going through the village of Abington and was approaching a point where the road took a sharp turn to the right. I saw a group of motorcyclists standing by the roadside. They flagged me down just as I approached the bend and I hit my brakes, resulting in the wheels going from under me. I slid off the scooter, landing in the middle of the busy main road. A truck came round the corner and missed me by inches and a car which had been behind me had to swerve to the left into a side road, narrowly missing me. If he'd swerved to the right he would have been in a head-on collision with the truck heading north. Fortunately I wasn't injured apart from some bruises and grazes. Two of the motorcyclists came and helped me off the road and another rescued my scooter.

I said, 'Why on earth did you flag me down?'

They said, 'There's oil on the road and we wanted to warn you, but we were too late.'

Nurses' Christian Fellowship

The evangelical Christian church I came from placed a lot of emphasis on *witnessing*. That is, taking every opportunity to speak to others about the Christian Gospel with the aim of making converts. In the building industry this was easy because as soon as they knew I was a practising Christian they would challenge me with questions about my beliefs. In general they knew they were *sinners* and were perfectly happy with that but they wanted to justify their lifestyle.

In nursing it was very different. There was a reluctance to discuss religion which was considered to be a private matter. This was to some extent because, as nurses, we must respect our patients' religious beliefs, and not do or say anything which could be seen as imposing our beliefs on them.

During the early months in nursing I was frequently asked why I'd made the change from building to nursing and I had to explain my objections to military service in relation to my Christian beliefs. This made it clear that I was a practising Christian and I very quickly realised that, as far as possible, I must live in a true Christian manner. The example of my parents came in here when I recalled that my father's main witness was preaching to people whereas my mother's witness was living as she believed Christ would have her live, by doing good to people. My father's method had worked for me in the building industry but now my mother's method was more appropriate.

When I was halfway through the training a student nurse who was about a year my junior made herself known to me. This was Doris Clews, a member of East Kilbride Baptist Church and a very enthusiastic Christian.

She told me, 'There's quite a number of Christians among the students and qualified staff. I feel we need to be able to get together for fellowship and mutual support, especially those of us who have to be resident.' It was the general rule that student nurses had to be resident but the rule was relaxed for male students due to the limited accommodation for males. Although qualified staff generally lived at home there were some who lived in.

I said, 'Do you have something in mind?'

'Yes,' she replied, 'I'd like to start a Nurses' Christian Fellowship. There was one here in the past but it fell through due to insufficient numbers. But I think we have the numbers to make it work now. I'm friendly with a past president and she can come and give us a talk on setting one up. There's a communal area in the Sisters' Home which would be ideal. I've made enquiries and we can have it one evening per month for our meetings.' This was clearly a girl on a mission so, more from a sense of responsibility than real enthusiasm, I agreed.

Our first meeting was arranged for the following month and we gathered in the Sisters' Home. The former president, who by then was a staff midwife in Glasgow, gave an inspirational talk and we had a discussion and vote. The majority wanted to go ahead. During the tea break I met a lot of people I didn't know were practising Christians and some whose lifestyles were quite the opposite of what I would have expected. After the tea break we discussed and voted on office bearers and I was nominated and seconded as president. This was a surprise to me since clearly the driving force was Doris and she would have been an ideal president. I suspect there was an element of sexism in the decision, since most Christian communities put women in a subordinate position to men at that time, and some still do. Again from a sense of duty rather than enthusiasm I accepted.

Things went fairly well for a few months but many soon drifted away and on occasions I would get a call from Doris to say, 'There's not enough coming this evening, you go round the male quarters and round them up and I'll go round the female quarters.' One by one they made excuses and we did struggle on for some months, but it became embarrassing when invited speakers turned up to only three or four members. Sadly we had to call it a day.

Enjoyable Hard Work

Nursing was as physical as bricklaying but I thoroughly enjoyed the work and learning new skills. I remember before I had the scooter standing in the queue for the bus at High Blantyre and feeling sorry for all those other people who were going to work in factories in East Kilbride. Nursing training at that time was very much along the lines of an apprenticeship with most of the training being work on the wards or in the theatre under the supervision of the ward sister. We had practical experience workbooks which were signed by the sisters as we learned new procedures and showed ourselves to be proficient. There were also blocks of classroom teaching when we were taught more advanced aspects, always followed by an examination.

As I recall we rotated through different areas of nursing in blocks of between two and three months. These were: urology; general surgery; general medicine; orthopaedics; paediatrics; thoracic medicine; ear, nose and throat; theatre; out-patients, A&E and night duty. Male nurses were not allowed in female wards so gynae-cology was theory only. Hairmyres Hospital didn't have dermatology or ophthalmology wards so we went out to the Victoria Infirmary, Glasgow for two months' derma-tology and to Glasgow Eye Infirmary for two months' ophthalmology. The scooter was extremely useful for this travelling.

While working in Glasgow Eye Infirmary, one day I had a problem with my sight. The vision in my left eye became blurred and I had difficulty seeing properly. When I looked in the mirror my left pupil was very large (dilated), and I thought I must have a serious eye condi-tion. Being in the Eye Infirmary there were specialist eye doctors around so I waited till the ward round was over when the consultant had gone and then I told a registrar about my problem.

He examined my eyes carefully and then he said, 'Have you been working with any kind of eye drops?'

I thought for a moment and answered, 'I was sent to empty bottles and wash them yesterday.'

'Do you know what was in the bottles?' he asked.

'Atropine.'

'That's what's wrong with your eye,' he said. 'You must have had some on your finger and rubbed your eye. I'm afraid you're stuck with it for four or five days but it will eventually wear off.' That was a relief and a lesson well learned.

A Route to Promotion

When I started nursing training at Hairmyres Hospital my only formal educational qualification was the City and Guilds Certificate in Bricklaying. I had left school at fifteen years of age with no qualifications and although I'd done two of the three years at night school studying for the Ordinary National Certificate in Building Technology, I left the building industry before completing it. Experience at School of Building showed me that I enjoyed studying and that was even more the case in nursing.

Nursing training was similar to an apprenticeship with most of the learning done on the wards but with periods in the school of nursing and an examination at the end of each study block. There were periods when no studying was required and I began to think about my future. What openings would be available to me after completing my training and what were the opportunities for promotion? After all I would get married and need to be able to earn more than a staff nurse's salary.

Most of the girls did midwifery after their general training, and very few were promoted without two nursing qualifications. Some would get married and leave the profession, at least for a time. Some would be promoted to Ward Sister and a very few, usually unmarried ladies, would go on to senior management posts such as supervisor, assistant matron, deputy matron or matron. Although there were males in these posts in psychiatric nursing I wasn't aware of any males in general nursing in Scotland.

There was one area where I was aware of a male nurse in a senior post and that was as a tutor. After gaining the necessary experience I could apply for the two-year course at Edinburgh University to do the nurse tutors' course. This in turn required university entrance educational qualifications.

There were two ways of funding the course. It could be done as a student in the usual way with a grant, or by secondment from a training hospital. In this case the hospital paid for the university fees and continued to pay a salary during the training. This normally required a commitment to return to the parent hospital and work as a tutor for a minimum of two years. The one big drawback with this route to promotion was similar to all other routes to promotion in nursing. Any promotion beyond charge nurse was promotion away from direct patient care and I didn't like that idea.

Educational Qualifications

With promotion in mind, about halfway through my training, I decided to start working for the necessary educational qualifications. There was no hurry since I still had one and a half years of my basic nursing training to go. Conditions for entry to the tutors' course, in addition to the educational qualifications, required at least four years' post-registration experience. Of these, at least three years must be as a sister or charge nurse in a training hospital. The Scottish system involved O grades and Highers. How to study was the next question. Night classes were out because of my shifts in nursing, and going to a further education college was out for the same reason, so I looked at the possibility of correspondence courses. There were a few around but all were designed for the English system, although some were prepared to adapt them for Scotland. I opted for the English system which involved GCE O levels and A levels. The next decision was what subjects to study.

A Dream

As I thought about this a crazy idea began to develop in my mind. I had thought of being a doctor as a child but that idea was firmly quashed. Perhaps I could study to be a doctor after all. But that's absurd with my background and education, or lack of it, I thought. I have a City and Guilds Certificate in Bricklaying and that's it. Besides, my mother's words were ringing in my ears, 'People like us can't be doctors. We don't have the brains for that.'

A poem by another Blantyre bricklayer and poet is relevant.

Quest of Life

It's my belief that everyone
Should go on the quest of life
To find that missing link
That vacant part of life

If it's your burning desire
To climb a mountain top
Strive to reach that peak
Go on and never stop

Everyone has a part in them
That yearns to reach their goal
A deep desire within themselves
That comes from within their soul

So carry out life's long dreams
And fulfil what's in your head
For if you don't, you'll have regrets
As they say, 'You're a long time dead'.

J. J. Whelan

Although learning a trade was the pinnacle of my mother's expectations for me, she was very pleased and proud of me when I made the change to nursing. On one occasion when she was with my father on a preaching engagement in another town, after the service they went to supper with a local family. The hostess had a son at university studying medicine, and she was very proud of his achievement to the extent of sounding boastful. My mother was a little irritated by her boasting, so she stuck out her very ample chest, pulled herself up to her full 5ft 2in. height, and proudly announced that her son was studying to be a nurse. I don't think the lady was very impressed but it gave my mother a lot of satisfaction.

Going round a bookshop looking for material to help with my education I found a little book entitled *Becoming a Doctor*. Aimed at secondary school pupils, it advised on what was needed; what subjects would be required, the kind of grades expected, where the medical schools were and what the course would be like. It was a bit daunting but the thought would not go away so I shared it with Mary. We discussed how long it was likely to take and what the financial implications would be. She was supportive so we devised a Plan A and a Plan B.

The suppression of my ambition in childhood still had its effects and I didn't have any confidence I could do it. Usually Plan B is in case Plan A fails but we decided to put that in reverse. I would work towards a realistic Plan A, the tutors' course, but keep Plan B in reserve as a remote possibility; *my dream*. I read the regulations for university entrance and then decided on my subjects. The requirements were English, a foreign language, maths, physics, chemistry and biology. I chose Latin as my foreign language since, I thought, doctors needed to know Latin.

I contacted a well-known correspondence college and the rep came to see me. He tried to dissuade me from studying medicine because it was unrealistic. He said, 'Why don't you try physiotherapy or radiography or something like that?'

I said, 'No, I'm preparing to do the tutors' course but, even if it is unrealistic, I want to keep my dream of being a doctor alive.' We decided on English and Latin as a start but that soon became a disaster on two fronts. Firstly Latin was too difficult to do on my own with no one for me to hear speaking the language and no one to listen to my speaking the words, and secondly I didn't like the methods of that particular correspondence college. They used text books that were not specific to the curriculum, and gave advice on which parts of the books to study. Separate notes were supplied for the parts of the curriculum that weren't covered in the books. This is a strategy used by many distance-learning organisations, but it involved a lot of unnecessary reading, and since I'd found at school that reading was hard work, I needed a new strategy.

After a little more research I discovered that I didn't need Latin and any foreign language would do. I changed to French since I had done some French at school and could get a Linguaphone course to listen to the language being spoken. After some further searching I found a correspondence college with a rather cheap-sounding name but decided to give them a go. This was The Rapid Results College. They didn't use any text books but instead prepared all their own teaching material tailored exactly to the curriculum and this worked well for me.

Nursing itself required study so I would put my more general studies to the side during study blocks and concentrate on them between blocks. But of course I was still working full-time and with fairly long and awkward hours. The split shifts we worked on some days wasted a lot of time. We worked in the morning, had the afternoon off and then came back on duty for the evening on those days. I decided to make use of this time for study.

Temptation

When I was halfway through my final year of nursing training I met Jack, a former apprentice I knew from the School of Building. After completing his National Service he started his own building business and was doing well. He had a contract for a project which would require him to hire another bricklayer and invited me to join him for this one job. It would take about a week and, because I had a week's holiday coming up, I agreed.

Going back to my old trade made an enjoyable change, and the money I earned made me realise just how much I was missing financially by being in nursing. Jack said he was expecting more work, and invited me to work for him on a permanent basis.

This was tempting. I could start earning good money and not have to look forward to years of living on a pittance in nursing. Having fulfilled the terms of my conditional registration as a conscientious objector, I was free to leave. Perhaps I could take this job and go back to night school to complete the National Certificate in Building Technology. I could think of starting my own business later.

I told Jack I would think about his offer and give him an answer in a week. On returning to the hospital after my short interlude, I was assigned to the children's ward. I went from building walls to learning how to change nappies and feed babies. Seeing and caring for ill children was emotionally challenging but very rewarding and I knew that hands-on patient care was for me despite the severe financial penalties. I let Jack know I wouldn't be joining him.

Interestingly, the staff nurse in the children's ward was married to an architectural technician and they had just recently built their own bungalow. He had drawn up the plans and together they did almost all of the physical building work. They found it a very satisfying experience and it gave me the idea that perhaps, one day, with my building experience, I could do the same. I never did.

Sexism

I mentioned the probable sexism in choosing me, a male, over a more suitable female, as president of the Nurses' Christian Fellowship. Sexism in medicine was rife at that time. The number of females admitted to medical school was restricted and opportunities for promotion severely limited. It still exists today but to a lesser extent.

There was certainly sexism too in the other direction in nursing in the 1950s and 1960s. In Scotland the big city teaching hospitals wouldn't take males for nursing training at all, no matter how many Highers they had. Indeed it was only in 1951 that males were allowed to become registered; Registered General Nurse (RGN) in Scotland and State Registered Nurse (SRN) in England. Now in the late 1950s and early 1960s it was left to the peripheral hospitals that had more difficulties with recruitment, and needed male students to make up their numbers.

We weren't allowed in female wards and our only contact with conscious female patients was during our periods in the Outpatient Department and Accident and Emergency. However, on night duty in my final year I was put in charge of an ENT ward with women and children. This was a first. Ear, Nose and Throat wards were considered low risk; after all it was mainly children having their tonsils removed and experienced auxiliary nurses were considered adequate on night duty. Tragically a child died following a tonsillectomy in such a ward with no qualified or student staff, so the decision was made to have a senior student in charge at night.

Male student nurses weren't allowed in the general theatre because gynaecological operations were carried out there and Matron considered it inappropriate that we should see these. We had to get our theatre experience in the thoracic and ENT theatres. ENT surgery was usually unexciting, but we did get valuable experience in the cardiothoracic theatre.

Sister was very good at getting us close to the action and usually asked the consultant cardiothoracic surgeon, Mr Dickie, if her students could scrub up and stand right up close to the action. At my first operation he appeared rather grumpy and was clearly not in the mood for such distractions but said, 'I suppose if you want him to, he can.' She signalled for me to go and scrub up. After the obligatory prolonged scrubbing of hands and forearms I donned the sterile gown, cap, mask, boots and sterile gloves, and stood up against the operating table next to the registrar, Mr Thomson, who was going to be assisting. My role was simply to observe and keep out of the way.

The patient, Mrs Inglis, had mitral stenosis, a narrowing of the mitral valve between the two chambers on the left side of the heart. I had met her in the ward when doing her case study and found her to be a very pleasant and helpful lady. She had a marked flush on her cheeks and became very breathless on even slight exertion.

Mr Dickie made the incision and removed a rib, and then the ribs were pulled apart to let him get to the heart. All the internal cutting was done with electrocautery to reduce bleeding, so there was a strong smell of burning flesh. The heart was beating throughout but the muscles that control breathing had been paralysed and the blood kept oxygenated artificially. A small incision was made in the heart and an instrument known as a

Tubbs mitral valve dilator inserted to stretch the narrowed valve. A special purse-string suture was put in place by the registrar and as the instrument was removed he was instructed to pull the suture tight to close the wound.

As the instrument was removed there was considerable bleeding from the heart wound and Mr Dickie shouted at the registrar, 'Pull harder, you need to tighten the suture more.' Mr Thomson pulled harder on the suture and even more blood spurted out with every heartbeat. The consultant was getting increasingly flustered and shouted at the registrar again, telling him to increase the tension on the suture. It didn't help, and blood kept pumping out. The anaesthetist, now worried by the blood loss and falling blood pressure, increased the speed of the blood transfusion and sent for more blood.

Now Mr Dickie composed himself and realised he needed another pair of hands. I was given suction apparatus and saline to suck the blood out of the chest cavity and then wash it out with saline to give a clear view while he inspected the wound. As I continued with the suction the blood continued to pump from the heart, but it gradually cleared enough to allow him to see what was going on. He discovered that the suture had been pulled too tightly to begin with, cutting the heart muscle, so that every time he told his registrar to pull harder it made it worse. Frantically he and Mr Thomson set to work putting in new sutures, and gradually the bleeding stopped and the patient's blood pressure slowly recovered.

When the operation was almost safely over, the consultant left his registrar to suture the final skin wound. He thanked Sister for her assistance as he normally did. Then he added, 'I reluctantly agreed to your nurse scrubbing up, but we'd never have managed without him.' Not a word was said to me but the fact that he said it in my presence was thanks enough, and more importantly it was gratifying to know I had helped, in a small way, to save a patient's life. I went back to see Mrs Inglis as part of my case study and she made a good recovery with marked improvement in her quality of life, but she remained blissfully unaware of the drama during her surgery.

On another occasion, when a patient with lung cancer was having part of his lung removed, Mr Dickie cut into the organ and a quantity of oily liquid appeared. This wasn't something I expected and since he was in a much better mood than on the previous occasion I asked him what it was.

'That's liquid paraffin.' I knew what liquid paraffin was, because it was part of my mother's medicine armoury and we were often given it to prevent constipation. I didn't like it but it was better than the dreaded castor oil.

I asked, 'How did it get into the lung?' Liquid paraffin is swallowed and goes into the digestive tract as a stool softener.

Mr Dickie replied, 'Because it's oily, a little trickles into the trachea when it's swallowed and with continued use, makes its way into the lung. I see this often; it should be banned.'

During our dermatology block in the Victoria, the consultant, Dr McPhater, had a patient with an interesting condition he wanted to show the student nurses. He was a highly regarded and very kind and popular doctor. The lesion was on a lady's knee so we all went into the consulting room to see this, but he went out to speak to the sister and she called me out. I was not to be allowed to see this because I was male. I felt humiliated since I was the only male student nurse there.

Sister spoke to me afterwards and apologised. She said, 'He asked me to tell the orderly to leave. When I explained that you're not an orderly but a student nurse he said, "Men are orderlies, not nurses."' He had served in the Royal Army Medical Corps during the war and his attitude was a throwback to then. This was an attitude I encountered on several occasions during my years in nursing, including from my own GP. When I attended him at the time I had required surgery he was very pleasant, acknowledging that I was on the hospital staff, and said, 'I see you're an orderly in Hairmyres.'

'No, I'm a student nurse,' I responded.

His reply? 'Women are nurses and do the real nursing, men assist them as orderlies.'

The ultimate indignity came after our final examinations. During the three-year training I had won first prize in most subjects and had excellent ward reports. It was generally expected that I would win the gold medal as the best student in the final year. However, just before the prize-giving Miss Sclater, the senior tutor called me to her office and apologised, telling me I wouldn't be getting the gold medal. She told me clearly that she and her fellow tutor thought I'd earned it but Matron had decided that another, female student should get it, but they had created a new runner-up medal just for me. It looked almost identical to the gold medal but in addition to my name had the words 'proxime accessit for gold medal'. I was puzzled and disappointed but accepted her explanation.

It wasn't till after I was charge nurse in another hospital that I learned the truth from someone who was friendly with Miss Sclater. There were two reasons why Matron refused to award me the gold medal. It had been a male nurse who won the gold medal in the two previous years and Matron was adamant she was not going to have a male win it three years in a row.

The second reason was related to my being a conscientious objector and the background of Helen to whom she awarded it. Helen was more mature than the rest of us. She had been a nurse in the war and had been given the status of SEN in recognition of her service and experience gained. Being highly regarded by the sisters she worked with she was persuaded to do additional training to gain the RGN qualification. Although she'd struggled academically, she did successfully complete the course and with very good ward reports. Her service to her country should now be rewarded with the gold medal. It had been a very stormy meeting with the tutors objecting strongly but when Matron pulled rank they accepted it on condition that a one-off *proxime accessit* medal be created for me.

Helen was a lovely person and, to her credit, felt embarrassed at the award. The first time I saw her after the decision was at the graduation ceremony when those of us who were receiving prizes sat together at the front of the hall. I congratulated her on her award and she replied, 'I'm sorry, Jimmy, this should have been yours and we all know it.' I assured her she was a worthy winner.

Four Wheels

Towards the end of my training at Hairmyres my brother John bought a scooter of the same make and model as mine. One day on his way to work he was involved in a serious collision with a car and was almost killed. He had multiple fractures to his face, skull and limbs and was taken unconscious to Law Hospital in Lanarkshire, but later transferred to Glasgow Royal Infirmary. He had many operations and had his jaw and facial bones wired up with his head in a metal frame for months, but did eventually recover. However, now our mother was terrified of us on two wheels and persuaded me to get rid of my scooter.

Since my training was almost at an end and I would be earning a bit more as a staff nurse, I traded my scooter in for a second-hand car. It was a Ford Prefect, two-tone blue and grey with an external sun visor. This time I took driving lessons before buying the car so was ready to drive right away.

Image 7-3: My Ford Prefect car outside our council house, 13 Cowan Wilson Avenue.

Having a car instead of the scooter made travelling more comfortable, especially for Mary. On the scooter I was fairly well sheltered from the wind and rain by the large windshield in front of me, but the pillion passenger had very little protection, so we'd limited our winter travelling to local runs. After getting the car we went out in all weathers, summer and winter. We had a week's holiday at Wanlockhead that first summer with the car and were able to tour the south of Scotland in comfort.

One winter's day we went to Wanlockhead to visit Aunt Jean. There had been some rain and the roads were wet but the rain went off. We spent a pleasant couple of hours and had a meal with her. Being near midwinter it was dark by this time and to our surprise when we emerged from the house to go home, the wet roads had frozen over and it was snowing, although there was only a light covering of snow.

We drove out of Fraser Terrace where Aunt Jean lived and there was a steep incline of about 70 yards to get on to the main road. The car wheels were spinning on the ice and we only made it halfway up the hill before having to reverse into the terrace and try again. Aunt Jean brought out a couple of rugs and ashes from the ash bin and threw them in front on the wheels. This was better but the wheels still spun and she said, 'I don't think it's wise to go on, you need to stay here overnight. This will get worse.'

The problem was we had no means of letting my parents know we wouldn't be home. Mary's parents had a telephone but mine did not and I remembered how frantic they were that time when I'd walked from Larkhall and arrived home in the early hours. Since John's accident they were even more prone to worry. Furthermore I was to be on duty in the morning, so I said, 'I must get home tonight, Aunt Jean, we'll keep trying.'

I was the only driver so Mary and Aunt Jean got behind the car and pushed. Slowly, slowly we crawled up the hill and on to the main road. This was on the level and there'd been some traffic so it appeared driveable, although I was aware that there was a steep hill to be climbed at the north end of the village going towards Leadhills. If we made that it would be downhill much of the way and any inclines wouldn't be as steep as this one until we reached the main A74 at Abington.

We stopped at the side of the road and Aunt Jean said, 'There are some things you need for the journey.' She took us back to the house where she filled a hot-water bottle and gave us some blankets and a shovel, and then we set off again.

Reaching the foot of the hill we began the ascent as steadily as possible. The car skidded a few times and halfway up the hill the wheels started spinning again and we came to a halt. There was no way of reversing to take another run at it because of the sharp bend on the lower part of the hill and we were in the middle of the road, blocking it. After fifteen minutes or so there were two more cars behind us, also stuck. The drivers of the other cars and Mary tried to push, but to no avail. Soon a Land Rover came over the hill from Leadhills and we were blocking his way too. Having four-wheel drive he had a better grip. He towed me up the hill and we were on our way again. He had to do the same for the other two cars. Whether or not he was happy about it didn't matter; it was the only way he could continue his journey.

It was still snowing and getting heavier as we con-tinued downhill to Leadhills where we had the option of continuing on the direct route to Abington and the A74 or turning off to the right and taking the slightly longer route through the village of Elvanfoot. Roads through hill country by their nature go up hill and down dale. Although the route through Elvanfoot was longer and the road narrower it had the slight advantage of featuring fewer inclines than the wider, direct route. In the end, we decided on the direct route to Abington simply because it was the main road. After leaving Leadhills we saw there were no car tracks, but we were making steady progress so continued downhill. Then the wind started to blow and the snow began to drift, building up into banks by the side of the road and drifting on to the carriageway. That was when we realised we'd made a mistake.

As we continued down into the valley we reached the point where a narrower road goes off to Crawford John, a small farming village up in the hills. It's a single-track road that climbs steeply up the side of the hill. The Wanlockhead folks had a saying: 'Out of the world and on to Crawford John.' We could see that this road was already blocked by a snowdrift, but the road end afforded us a place where it would have been possible to turn round and go back to Leadhills. But we knew this wasn't feasible because there was no way we'd have been able to get back up the hill, so we had no option but to continue: but not for long. We soon ran into a snowdrift completely blocking the road and were well and truly stuck. The shovel we had was useless against this amount of snow so we just had to sit and wait.

At this point I remembered photographs we'd seen during our childhood holidays of snowdrifts right up to the cottage roofs with the adults dwarfed beside them. We should have taken Aunt Jean's advice because she clearly knew these hills and valleys, but thanks to her foresight we were at least able to keep warm. Mary and I snuggled up together and wrapped ourselves in the blankets. It would have been quite romantic if it hadn't been so very frightening. We felt so alone in the dark with the wind howling across the valley and the snow building up against the car.

After about two hours of this we saw headlights in the distance and coming towards us. They disappeared but reappeared nearer to us. We waited and hoped it would be a snowplough and sure enough after a further five minutes, that's what arrived and the men stopped and helped to dig us out. We were freed and able to get on our way to Abington and the main A74, which was always kept open. On reaching Abington we found a telephone kiosk and telephoned Mary's parents to reassure them. The journey was uneventful from there and as we reached the bleak Douglas Moor there was no snow; only wind and rain.

When we arrived in Blantyre my parents were beginning to get anxious, but since we were there before midnight they weren't too worried because it was frequently well after 11 pm when I came home after being out with Mary. We learned later that the snowplough had come up Mennock Pass and through Wanlockhead about forty-five minutes after we left, and on reaching Leadhills had taken the road through Elvanfoot to the A74 before coming back up the direct route where they met us. If we'd taken Aunt Jean's advice to stay overnight we would have seen the snowplough go past. We could then have changed our minds and followed it all the way to the A74, and avoided the scary experience.

The Next Step

As my training was coming to an end I had to decide what to do next. Staying on as a staff nurse was an option but having only one nursing qualification was a disadvantage for future promotion. Most of the girls did midwifery but that wasn't open to males and I had no interest in it in any case. Some of the male student nurses had trained in psychiatric nursing before coming to general and I did consider that and training for the RMN (Registered Mental Nurse) qualification or for the RNMD (Registered Nurse for Mental Defectives)—later changed to RLDN (Registered Learning Difficulties Nurse). However I wasn't very interested and would only have been doing it for the qualification.

My final ward experience was in the Orthopaedic Ward and this was the first time I'd encountered orthopaedics. The charge nurse, the title for a male nurse with an equivalent ranking to sister, made it interesting and discussed the technicalities of pulleys, weights and angles in relation to traction. He told me about the Orthopaedic Nursing Certificate, and that he had done his orthopaedic training at Killearn Hospital in a rural part of Stirlingshire.

'You could do your training there,' he said. It was at a considerable distance from home but since I had the car it was manageable, so I decided to do that.

The written, final state registration examination was held in our own hospital with external invigilators in attendance, but the practical and oral had to be taken at another hospital. In our case it was the Victoria Infirmary, Glasgow. The examiner was very kind and as a final question asked me something about Florence Nightingale. I said I was aware of her importance in the history of nursing but couldn't answer that specific question.

She replied, 'Never mind, now that you've passed your exams you'll have more time for reading about the history of nursing.' I didn't think anything of her comment at the time but as I walked out of the hospital I thought, she just said I've passed my exams; can she mean that?

After getting the results there was a graduation ceremony when we were presented with the prizes we'd

Image 7-4: Prize-giving and graduation Hairmyres Hospital 1962. I am third from right on front row.

won in the final year, and I received my runner-up medal with my other prizes. We were registered with the General Nursing Council and I was now James Graham RGN.

Matron called each of us to her office for a chat about our plans for the future. I informed her I was going to apply to do the Orthopaedic Nursing Certificate course at Killearn Hospital.

Image 7-5: Miss Hardie.
Courtesy of NHS Greater Glasgow
and Clyde Archives (HD 28/12/18).

She answered, 'That's excellent, but why do you want to go away out to Killearn? The Victoria Infirmary has an Orthopaedic Nursing Certificate course and most of your training would be done at Philipshill Hospital. It's only a couple of miles down the road and I'm friendly with the matron. If you're interested I'll recommend you to her.'

This was a surprise to me, firstly because she'd knocked me back for the gold medal, and secondly because I'd assumed the Victoria Infirmary was an all-female nursing establishment. She assured me that since I wouldn't be a student nurse but a staff nurse doing a post-registration course, being male would not be a barrier. This was good news to me and I agreed to her suggestion. She arranged an interview and I went along armed with my application form. On this occasion I had no problem with referees since the matron and senior tutor were both very happy to provide references.

I should add that although I was a bit miffed at only getting a runner-up medal rather than the gold medal, I still felt I had a lot to be grateful for to Miss Hardie our matron. She had accepted me for nurse training as a raw lad straight off a building site with no relevant qualifications and little or no idea of what nursing really entailed, not to mention my two brilliant referees. Now she was giving me good advice regarding further training and supporting me in my application.

Chapter 8

Nursing at Philipshill Hospital

Staff Nurse

I was called to two interviews, one with the matron of Philipshill Hospital and one with the matron of the Victoria Infirmary. I was offered the post of staff nurse in post-registration training for the Orthopaedic Nursing Certificate.

Image 8-1: Architects' sketch of the proposed new Philipshill Hospital from 1925. The actual hospital was different in some respects but the layout of the wards was the same. Courtesy of NHS Greater Glasgow and Clyde Archives.

Philipshill Hospital was the orthopaedic unit of the Victoria Infirmary, Glasgow but separated from it by about six miles. It had its own matron who had a degree of autonomy, but was under the overall control of the matron at the Victoria. There were six wards originally but Ward 2 had been converted to physiotherapy and X-ray departments. The other five wards retained their original numbering. The wards all had verandas and some patients were nursed outside all the time, mainly those with tuberculosis of the bone and some with other bone infections such as osteomyelitis and septic arthritis. Some patients suffering from the late effects of polio-myelitis spent some time outside. Other patients were mainly those admitted for elective surgery, those requiring bed rest and trauma victims who had been admitted via A&E in the Victoria, stabilised and then transferred. In addition to orthopaedics there were ear, nose and throat operations and some plastic surgery. When I arrived on my first day I was instructed to report to Sister Park in Ward 5. She appeared delighted to have a full-time staff nurse and even more excited at having a male staff nurse. Having done her training in the Victoria and worked there as a staff nurse she had never seen a male nurse before, so I was taken on a tour of the wards so she could show off her new staff nurse to the other sisters. They were all very welcoming and although I felt a bit like a prize poodle, it was a pleasant introduction to my new hospital.

The training regime was much the same as at Hairmyres with most of the time on the wards but with a few weeks here and there in lectures. My practical experience was in the adult male and the children's wards, theatre,

A&E and the plaster room, these last two being at the Victoria.

The knowledge of anatomy required for orthopaedics was much more detailed than for general nursing, especially in relation to bones, muscles, tendons, ligaments and nerves. Nursing procedures specific to orthopaedics had to be learned. Many patients were nursed on metal frames on leather cushions and proper care of the leather was vital. Others were in plaster casts and some were on traction with pulleys and weights. They could be in this position for many weeks or months.

Engagement

Mary and I became engaged to be married on 1 January 1962 near the end of my general nursing training, and the wedding date was set for 6 September 1963. This would be some months after I was due to complete the orthopaedic nursing training, so after starting at Philipshill, I applied for a council house in the new town of East Kilbride. At that time housing allocation was controlled by the East Kilbride Development Corporation and priority was given to people in permanent employment in East Kilbride.

Miss Gunn, the deputy matron, came to me one day and said, 'I've received this form from the Development Corporation and they want to know how long you're going to be working here. Will I say, indefinite?'

I replied, 'Yes, thank you, that would be helpful. I don't know what will happen after I complete my training but I've no plans to leave at present.' We were subsequently allocated a flat but it wasn't going to be available till a few weeks after our marriage.

Promotion

Towards the end of my year Sister Park gave notice that she was leaving, so the post of Sister was to be advertised. Around that time I was doing a ward round with Miss Gunn and she asked, 'Why don't you apply for the post?'

'I didn't think there was any point,' I replied. 'I've been a staff nurse for less than a year, I haven't completed my orthopaedic training and I'm not due to sit the Certificate examination for another month.'

She answered, 'You'll have completed your training and sat the examination before Sister Park leaves. We think you would have a good chance of getting it.'

I applied and was called for an interview with Miss Locke, the matron of the Victoria Infirmary. She told me that Miss Whyte, the Philipshill matron, and Mr MacDougall, the senior consultant surgeon, thought I would do the job very well so after informing her that I was soon to be married I was appointed as Charge Nurse of Ward 5. I would be called Mr Graham.

Marriage

Under Scottish law when a couple are being married, notice has to be given publicly, either by having the notice read in a parish church, or by posting a notice outside the registrar's office in the place of residence for three weeks. Since I lived in Blantyre and Mary lived in Rutherglen we had our notices in different places, and we were being married in yet another place, Cambuslang. We had the notices posted in good time and collected our certificates from the registrar to say that the necessary notice had been provided.

Christian Brethren didn't have ministers but certain men within local churches took the title of *pastor* in order to conduct wedding ceremonies. We had arranged to be married by Bill Friel who was a member of the Cambuslang Brethren and also a full-time evangelist in the Brethren Movement. Two weeks before our wedding day he announced his intention to leave the Brethren and join the local Cambuslang Baptist Church forthwith, so would be unable to marry us. This left us having to hurriedly look for someone else in another Brethren Church, someone we didn't know and couldn't have much preparation time with. An old friend of Mary's parents', Mr Cormack, agreed to step in.

Our wedding day, 6 September 1963, was a Friday and when I arrived at the church, called Albert Hall, Mr Cormack asked me for the marriage licence so I handed him the two certificates we'd been given by the registrars.

He said, 'No, I need your marriage licence.'

'That's what we were given by the registrars.'

'You should have taken these to the registrar in Cambuslang and collected your marriage licence from there. I can't marry you without the licence.' There was hurried discussion and he agreed to perform the marriage ceremony but explained we wouldn't be legally married. Willie Samuels, a friend of Mary's family, took the certificates and hurried off to try to catch the registrar before the office closed, but we were not hopeful that he'd get there on time.

Meanwhile my bride arrived completely unaware of the drama and we went through the wedding ceremony with Mary thinking all was well and me thinking we were not actually being married. I had apparently turned pale at one point in the ceremony when I felt myself swaying and thinking I was about to faint. I remember it every time I see clips of grooms fainting at the altar on Harry Hill's *You've Been Framed*. However, I did get through it without fainting and then we went to the vestry.

The first thing was to tell Mary and then hope and pray. She in turn started to panic and there was no sign of Willie Samuels. Was that a good or a bad sign? As we waited nervously, we had a discussion about what we were going to do, and what we were going to say to the guests. The reception would go ahead as arranged. Silvertrees Hotel in Bothwell had been arranged a year in advance and a coach from Parks of Hamilton was waiting outside to take those guests without cars to the hotel, but there was a problem with the honeymoon. The marriage could not be legal till Monday after the registrar's office reopened and we would have to meet with Mr Cormack and the witnesses to do the necessary paperwork. Our plans were to stay at Mary's brother Roddy's house for two nights while he and his wife Theresa stayed with Mary's parents, and then we would fly to Austria on Sunday. The honeymoon would have to be cancelled since we couldn't afford to pay for a later flight and going

Image 8-2: Mary and I cutting the cake.

off on honeymoon unmarried was unthinkable.

Then Willie appeared looking red-faced and rather breathless, but with a big smile and waving a piece of paper. He had managed to get the required licence so we all signed on the dotted line and it was legal. We were married.

A friend had an 8mm cine camera and he made a short film of our wedding. Recently when clearing out a shed I discovered a polythene bag full of old 35mm slides and 8mm film, including that of our wedding. Despite being over fifty years old and having survived many house moves and storage in lofts, garages and sheds the films have survived and I've had them digitised. They're not the same quality as modern digital videos but still give an adequate flavour of the time. I have the wedding film on a YouTube video on my website: www.ascottishdoctor.com/nursing-philipshill-hospital.

Our honeymoon was in the Austrian Tyrol, in the little village of Obsteig, which we thoroughly enjoyed. We've both had a love of Austria since then. On our return to Scotland we didn't have a home of our own ready to go to but Mary's parents kindly let us stay with them until it was ready a few weeks later. Our two-bedroom flat was on the third floor at 30 Dick's Park, East Kilbride.

Married Life

Settling in to married life had its ups and downs. My Ford Prefect car was proving too expensive to run and now we had our own home with rent, rates and electricity bills, plus the cost of furnishing it, the car was a luxury we could no longer afford, so it was sold. Travelling for me was easy since it was only two miles, a few minutes' bus ride, to Philipshill and I often walked home. Mary on the other hand had a much longer journey than previously. I worked a split shift about twice a week, so was home in the afternoon when Mary was at work and out at work in the evening when she was at home.

Since I often worked at weekends I had a day and a half off midweek and tried to help with the housework. My first attempt at helping with the laundry resulted in whites coming out of the washing machine pink. Rewashing with lots of extra detergent didn't help. They remained pink and I remained skint for some time till I'd replaced all the whites.

On another occasion we were having liver for our evening meal and I decided to fry the liver for when she came home. I had seen Mary use a tenderiser on steak. This is a heavy sort of hammer with coarse spikes. Of course I would need to tenderise the liver and set about hammering it with this implement. Mary came home to find the kitchen covered in blood and thought I'd been attacked by a mad axe murderer. Lesson One: don't wash coloureds and whites together; Lesson Two: don't tenderise liver.

Mary's biggest disaster from my point of view was giving me pilchards. She bought a tin of the fish, and never having had them herself, thought they would be interesting. I took a couple of bites and I think they tasted fine but the more I looked at these creatures with their lifeless eyes staring back at me, the more my stomach began to heave, and eventually I threw up. I have never touched a pilchard since, and even as I type I can feel that stirring in the pit of my stomach as I think of them.

Charge Nurse

After passing the examination for the Orthopaedic Nursing Certificate I could call myself James Graham RGN ONC. I settled into the routine of being a charge nurse and running my own ward. On day duty I was in charge of a full-time staff nurse, a part-time staff nurse, usually four or five student nurses, three auxiliary nurses and a domestic. At night the ward was staffed by a staff nurse and an auxiliary nurse.

One of my first daily duties after taking the report from the night staff nurse was to go round the ward and speak briefly to each patient asking them what sort of night they'd had, and answer any question they had about the coming day. The staff were excellent dedicated nurses and knew their duties, which they performed diligently while creating a happy atmosphere for the patients. This was important since many were there, often in plaster, frames or traction, for months.

Motivating and earning loyalty from staff was one of my main aims. I think I succeeded in this because on one occasion I was speaking to a student nurse who had just come over from the Victoria Infirmary on her first ward assignment after Preliminary Training School. She said she'd been asked which ward she was coming to and answered, 'Ward 5.'

The other nurse responded, 'That's the holiday camp.'

I felt rather disappointed that I was regarded as being lax in discipline but my staff nurse, who overheard the conversation and probably saw my face, told me, 'That's a compliment. You create a generally happy atmosphere in the ward and they enjoy coming to Ward 5. They work as hard as they do in any other ward, but more from a sense of loyalty rather than fear.' That made me feel better because it was my duty to make sure they did their work, but I could always trust them to get on with it.

There was one occasion however which I'm ashamed of and feel I let myself down very badly. I came in one morning feeling grumpy. I can't remember why, and although first thing in the morning was never my best time I usually kept my feelings to myself. I walked into the ward and the night staff nurse and auxiliary nurse were standing in the middle of the ward. One was facing one side and the other the opposite side of the ward waving their arms like conductors while all of the patients were singing like a choir.

It should have filled me with pride but instead I became very angry and shouted up the ward, 'What do you think you're doing? This is a hospital ward, not a concert hall.' There was a sudden silence and immediately I realised I'd been an unreasonable fool. Staff nurse came to the duty room to give the night report and apologised but said, 'We weren't shirking though, we've completed all our duties.' It was my turn to apologise. After saying I was sorry, I thanked her and asked her to continue to do her best to make the patients' stay as happy as possible.

A considerable part of my working day was in the duty room doing ward administration. I was responsible for ward rounds with Matron or her deputy. Ward rounds with the consultants were an important responsibility, making sure laboratory and X-ray results were available, and reporting on progress. During visiting hours there would be a steady stream of visitors enquiring about the progress of their relatives.

Discouragement

Although I enjoyed my work as a charge nurse I went through a period of feeling discouraged. Someone like me was never going to manage to become a doctor and I had a long road ahead to become a nurse tutor. I still had a minimum of two and a half years more as a charge nurse while continuing to study for university entrance.

There would then be two years at Edinburgh University living on a grant, and what would Mary and I do? Would I live in student accommodation while she stayed on in East Kilbride, or would we give up our home here and look for a flat in Edinburgh?

Reading a nursing journal I saw an advert by a large pharmaceutical company, looking for people with nursing experience to talk to doctors about their products. Training would be provided. They were offering an excellent salary plus bonuses and a company car. It looked very attractive. I could give up all this studying and earn good money right away.

I applied and they called me for interview. The first interviewer asked, 'Why do you want to leave nursing?' Clearly I should have been ready with a list of all the positive aspects of the post on offer, but feeling in a discouraged frame of mind I gave a list of negatives such as the continuous studying, poor salary and awkward hours.

A second interviewer asked if I had any experience of selling and I replied, 'No.'

'How do you know you'll be able to sell our products?'

I fumbled the answer and said something like, 'Your advert said you were looking for people with nursing experience to talk to doctors about your products. I have plenty of experience of communicating with doctors.' The reality was beginning to dawn on me. They were looking for a salesperson, and I hadn't realised this because the advert said nothing about selling. How naive was I?

Needless to say I didn't get the job and I realised it wasn't for me in any case. Hands-on, patient care was what I enjoyed. I settled down to gaining the necessary experience and became reinvigorated to take up my general educational studies again.

Evolving Orthopaedics

Mr MacDougall was appointed senior consultant in charge of the Orthopaedic Department at the Victoria Infirmary and Philipshill Hospital shortly before my arrival and at this time the treatment and nursing of orthopaedic conditions were changing rapidly. Tuberculosis, poliomyelitis, osteomyelitis and septic arthritis had subsided but not disappeared. Rickets and osteomalacia due to vitamin D deficiency had almost disappeared but the long-term effects on bones still needed treatment. The treatment of injuries and osteoarthritis was evolving and we were one of the first places to introduce total hip replacement surgery.

Before this, patients with osteoarthritis of the hip had an operation called subtrochanteric osteotomy where the thigh bone was cut through just below the hip and reset in a slightly different position. In most cases this was held in position with a pin and plate and the patient put on traction with weights and pulleys and confined to bed for a couple of weeks. However one surgeon, Mr Norton, didn't like this pin-and-plate method and he put his patients in plaster for six weeks.

Imagine my surprise after our first hip replacement operation. I was instructed to get the patient out of bed and on to his feet the day following surgery. My staff nurse and I went very carefully and helped him to swing his legs out of bed, then slowly and gently on to the floor, fully expecting his hip to give way. No such thing happened as with a big beam on his face he took a few pain-free steps. The treatment of osteoarthritis of the hip had been transformed. Knee replacement surgery followed but it would be years before this had the consistently good results of hip replacement.

Spinal Injuries Unit

Mr MacDougall, affectionately known as Archie, visited the Miners' Rehabilitation Centre in nearby Uddingston regularly to give advice. Some of those patients had spinal cord injuries with paralysis, usually from the waist down (paraplegia), or more rarely from the neck down (quadriplegia). Apart from mining accidents, many patients with spinal injuries were victims of other industrial incidents and road accidents. Mr MacDougall realised there was a need for a facility dealing with all categories of spinal injury.

He set up a fledgling unit for the specialised treatment of these patients at Philipshill in Ward 4, in the efficient and dedicated care of Sister Alison McQueen. At first this consisted only of two or three beds, and was part of her general orthopaedic ward, but it gradually developed and became a dedicated regional spinal injuries unit. It was subsequently transferred to the Southern General Hospital, Glasgow as the Scottish National Spinal Injuries Unit where there is a Philipshill and an Edenhall Ward in recognition of the origins of the unit in the West and East of Scotland.

The enthusiasm of Archie and Alison for this project was unbounded, and they also developed an interest in what was then known as the Stoke Mandeville Games. These games had been started in 1948 for veterans of World War II with spinal injuries at Stoke Mandeville Hospital, Buckinghamshire, England. They gradually grew and became international and are now the Paralympic Games.

Alison McQueen was Sister of Ward 4 when I arrived in Philipshill and she had a reputation for being a very strict and humourless sister. She'd been in a stable and seemingly loving relationship with a naval officer and enjoyed a very glamorous lifestyle with him. They got engaged, but a few weeks before the wedding she discovered he was already married. She was devastated and became embittered for some time. However she soon overcame the bitterness but not the hurt and threw herself heart and soul into her work caring for her paralysed patients and developing the spinal injuries unit with Mr MacDougall. The 1964 Olympic Games were held in Tokyo, followed by the Paralympic Games also in Tokyo. I recall Alison's great enthusiasm for this and her zeal in recruiting volunteer nurses to accompany her wheelchair-bound patients who were participating in the games. Sadly Alison died prematurely of cancer but her dedicated work in Ward 4 Philipshill was pivotal in the development of the unit.

My personal involvement in the unit was limited to deputising when Alison was on holiday, giving lectures on the subject to groups of student nurses from other hospitals and helping out with occasional spells on night duty. One of my most abiding memories is of when I was doing the 10 pm ward round and was a little later than usual. We came to John, a young lad who had sustained a fracture dislocation of his cervical spine, the worst type of broken neck. John was quadriplegic, and although he was able to breathe without assistance, he had no power in any of his four limbs and no sensation below the neck. This meant that everything had to be done for him. Despite the horrendous implications, he was a remarkably pleasant and co-operative young man and we usually had a chat before I moved on to the next patient.

On this occasion we arrived at John's bed and he was completely covered by a woollen blanket. It was tightly wrapped around his head so I turned to the staff nurse and asked, 'What happened to John? Matron didn't mention this in her report, and why isn't he screened off?'

She looked at me strangely and said, 'John's fine. He's not dead, that's how he sleeps at night.'

I replied, 'You can't leave him like that, he'll suffocate. Please remove the blanket from his face.'

She protested, 'He always sleeps like that, but if you insist.'

When she removed the blanket from his face, John said, 'Hello, Mr Graham. Please let Nurse Gibson put the blanket over my face again. During the day I can see and hear what's going on around me, but in bed at night the only sensation I have is from the skin on my face.'

'That's all very well, John,' I answered, 'but I'm concerned that you may suffocate.' He assured me he

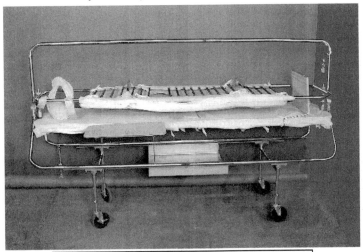

Image 8-4: An old Stryker turning frame.

wouldn't and always slept that way, so I apologised for disturbing him and agreed to his blanket. It made me realise just how awful it must be to have no sensation below the neck and a complete inability to move any limb.

I was able to observe the evolution of the unit as it changed from one or two patients on normal hospital beds in a general orthopaedic ward to a dedicated unit with specialised Stryker Turning Frames that could be turned with the patient sandwiched in them. These have continued to evolve and are now very sophisticated.

Image 8-4 is of an old Stryker Turning Frame. The patient lies on the lower part on his back facing upwards for two hours. When due to be turned the upper part is placed over him and he is strapped firmly between them. The apparatus is then rotated through 180° so that he is now lying on his face with forehead supported by a sling. After lying this way for two hours the procedure is reversed and he is turned back again. This is essential to prevent pressure sores and to prevent movement at the fracture site during turning. Another innovation was the Circle Electric Bed which allowed the patient to be rotated slowly towards a more upright position after a certain time in a horizontal position.

While searching for relevant images recently I made contact with Jim Hemauer. In 1970, as a fifteen-year-old from near Plymouth, Wisconsin, USA, he went diving with friends in a private diving hole. As he dived from a considerable height a friend's head bobbed out of the water just where he was aiming. Taking action to avoid a collision with his friend took him into shallow water and he hit the solid ground at speed rendering him uncon- scious and causing crush fractures of two cervical vertebrae with a resultant quadriplegia, paralysis of all four limbs.

Jim spent seven weeks on a Stryker Frame on trac- tion with weights pulling his head to prevent movement and further nerve damage while healing of the bones took place. I asked him how he felt on the Stryker Frame and especially when being turned.

He replied, 'My recollections are a little foggy, but what I do remember was that it was terribly uncomfortable. My head would get extremely sore because it rested only on a thin strap. It was also very confining. When they put the bed together to turn me, I remember feeling like I was a "sandwich". As they actually flipped me over, it was very frightening at first, but something I eventually got used to. It happened very quickly so it was over with fast. I hated being in that bed. Remember, I was fifteen years old, injured beyond my comprehension and very confused about everything that was going on.' After seven weeks on the Stryker Frame he graduated to the Circle Electric Bed and eventually to a normal hospital bed.

Jim made a partial recovery in that his fractures healed but he remains paralysed. Despite this, forty-five years on, he lives a fulfilled life with a loving wife and family, and works as Associate Director of the Disability Resource Centre at a US university.

He has kindly given me permission to provide this abbreviated account and to use images of him on the Stryker Frame and Circle Electric Bed on my website: www.ascottishdoctor.com/nursing-philipshill-hospital where I have also provided a link to his website. I recommend visiting this to see all Jim's images and read his inspirational story in full.

Man of the House

My first Christmas as Charge Nurse was interesting and a little disturbing. Having been in Accident and Emergency at the Victoria Infirmary the previous Christmas I was unaware of the Philipshill traditions. I understood my duties regarding decorating the ward and providing extras for the Christmas dinner such as special desserts, cakes and biscuits. The turkey dinner came from the hospital kitchen and was served from a table at one end of the ward almost as usual, or so I thought.

At the beginning of December one of the sisters asked me who was going to carve the turkey for me. I said, 'I'm not sure I know what you mean. I assume the turkey will come to the ward ready for plating as usual.'

She replied, 'No, we get a whole turkey and there's a tradition that each sister gets one of the consultants or senior doctors to carve it.' This caused a problem for me since they knew the ropes and made arrangements in early November, so those willing to give up this time on Christmas Day were already booked. I asked around the consultants, senior registrars, registrars and anaesthetists but none was available. Time was getting on and we were getting close to Christmas, so what was I to do? I mentioned my dilemma to one of the other sisters at dinner one evening and she replied, 'You don't need to ask a doctor to carve your turkey; you're a man.'

'Thank you for noticing,' I replied, 'but why does that make a difference?'

'The reason we ask them is because we're ladies and it's traditional for the man of the house to carve the turkey—and that's you.' Welcome to the mid twentieth century! But it was a relief, so on Christmas Day I took my place as head of the house and carved the turkey. Was this another example of sexism, but this time with women themselves perpetuating their subservient position?

There was a piano in each of the wards because

Image 8-5: The author with ward nurses, Christmas 1963.

many patients were long stay and we had a music teacher come in weekly. On Christmas Day after the dinner, Dr Seymour, the GP who did a daily round, came in and visited all of the wards and played the piano for half an hour or so in each ward. It was traditional to provide him with hospitality in the form of a regular supply of whisky, so after two to three hours of piano-playing his co-ordination became somewhat impaired!

I took a few photos of Christmas Day in the ward that year. The following Christmas I was more familiar with the routines and had several patients' relatives involved in the festivities. One was a chef who assisted with the Christmas dinner. Two had accordions and provided additional musical accompaniment. I had acquired a basic 8mm silent cine camera and made a short film which despite fifty years neglect has, like the film of my wedding, survived. I had it digitised and posted it on my website as a YouTube video: www.ascottishdoctor.com/nursing-philipshill-hospital.

A Promise

During my time at Philipshill, becoming a doctor was still only a dream and I was planning to be a tutor once I had the necessary experience. This was a minimum of four years post-registration, of which three must be in charge of a ward or department with responsibility for training student nurses.

At one point, when I had about eighteen months' experience as a charge nurse, the new hospital in Kilmarnock, Crosshouse Hospital, was advertising for clinical instructors. The use of clinical instructors was a new innovation, or experiment, in nurse-teaching at that time. The idea was that tutors would do classroom teaching as before but the clinical instructors would take groups of student nurses into the wards to teach them practical

279

procedures. This would relieve the ward sisters and charge nurses of some of the responsibility, and provide a more uniform level of teaching.

I decided to apply for one of the posts, thinking it would be a useful step up towards being a tutor and it would let me know if I enjoyed teaching. When I asked Miss Whyte, the matron of Philipshill, for a reference, she said she would provide one but didn't think it a very wise move. She suggested I speak to Miss Locke, the matron of the Victoria Infirmary, who was in overall control.

An appointment was made and I went to see Miss Locke. She asked me about my plans for the future and why I wanted to leave, so I told her I was hoping to become a nurse tutor and that getting some experience as a clinical instructor would be useful experience before going to Edinburgh University to take the nurse tutors' course. She disagreed and told me I would get far better experience continuing in my post as a charge nurse for the next eighteen months. 'If you do that,' she said, 'we'll second you to Edinburgh University to do the tutors' course.'

I was taken aback by this since the Victoria Infirmary didn't take male student nurses.

'That surprises me. Why would you be prepared to pay for my training when you don't take male students? Does this mean you'll be taking males in the near future?'

'No,' she said, 'we've no plans to admit male students but that doesn't mean we can't have a male tutor, and we would regard you as a very useful member of the teaching staff.' This was too good an offer to refuse so I thanked her, accepted and agreed to stay on at Philipshill.

I was still uncertain about my future, planning to be a nurse tutor but secretly hoping that I would make the grade and get into medical school.

A Blast from the Past

Shortly after this Miss Whyte, our matron, told me she had a male medical student who had just completed his first year and wanted some experience working with patients for two months during the summer holiday. She was taking him on as an auxiliary nurse for two months and he would be working with me in Ward 5. 'His name is Andrew Evans,' she said, 'and he'll report for duty on Monday morning.'

When he reported for duty I immediately recognised him as the same Andrew Evans who had been dismissed from Hairmyres Hospital. I said, 'I recognise you from Hairmyres.'

'Yes,' he replied, 'and I recognise you. You're Jimmy Graham.'

'That's right but it's Mr Graham while you're here and you are Nurse Evans. I don't suppose you told Miss Locke or Miss Whyte about your time in Hairmyres.'

'No, and I'd rather they didn't know.'

'That's fine with me,' I replied. 'Just make sure you keep your nose clean while you're here.'

To my surprise he worked well while with me and appeared keen to learn. During conversations with him, he told me what Miss Hardie, the Hairmyres matron had said to him. He'd thought, I'll show her I'm fit to be far more than a street sweeper. He explained, 'I enrolled at a further education college and worked hard for two years then re-sat all of my exams to get the grades I needed. So here I am—a medical student. When I graduate I'm going to apply for a post as a junior doctor in Hairmyres just so I can show her what I've achieved.'

This encounter made me more determined to try to get into medical school.

Try a Shortcut

By 1965 I had acquired my six O levels but still had another year before I could apply for entry to the tutor course. The thought occurred to me at this point: I have six O levels, a City and Guilds, an RGN and an Ortho-paedic Nursing Certificate; perhaps they might take them into account.

I decided to apply for entry to study medicine at Glasgow University but I wasn't telling anyone outside the family. While completing the form I realised I needed two references and one should be my school headmaster. This wasn't particularly relevant in my case since it was twelve years since I'd left school, but I made an appointment and went along to see him. He was polite but made it clear that he didn't think much of my chances. However he wrote me a reference outlining the subjects I had studied at school and saying that I'd done well in all my subjects.

Before my application could go to the University of Glasgow I needed a Certificate of Fitness from the Scottish Universities Entrance Board. They vetted all applications for entry to Scottish universities to ensure that qualifications were of the quality and quantity required, and they totally rejected me, not only for medicine but also for any university course.

Facing Reality

In one year's time I would have fulfilled the nursing criteria for entrance to the tutors' course. Converting two of my O levels would get me into that but I needed three to be even considered for medicine. I hadn't had any sense of urgency up to now and had taken a rather leisurely approach to my O levels. Given my history of timidity regarding the possibility of becoming a doctor, I should have been feeling discouraged following my rejection. On the contrary I thought, I want to do this next year, and I still want to be a doctor so I must do three A levels in the next year. This was a tall order since it takes two years' full-time study to take subjects from O level to A level.

I made some enquiries and found a small private school in Hillhead, Glasgow; Glasgow Tutorial College. The thought occurred to me that perhaps I could get a grant to study full-time and do the three A levels in one year, so I went to see the principal, a Dr Slack. He told me that I could do the studies with them but I would have to do it over two years, and it was unlikely I would get any kind of grant. Still determined to try to do it in one year, I went back to Rapid Results College and discovered they did courses for A levels in physics and chemistry but not biology—and I needed all three. However, after studying the curriculum for A level biology I found a textbook that followed the curriculum fairly closely. I decided on that. Meanwhile, I could continue to work full-time. Part-time work wasn't a financial option.

Since the examinations were held twice a year my plan was to do physics and chemistry in the first six months then biology in the second six months, but this would mean applying to university before sitting the biology exam.

There was one further hurdle. With O levels, apart from the oral examination in French, all the exams were written only. With A level science subjects there were practical laboratory examinations and we had to do practical laboratory work during the course, and have the work certified by the teacher.

This required a trip back to Glasgow Tutorial College and this time they were able to help. I could do two evenings per week laboratory work with their tutors, one for physics and one for chemistry for the first six months and then two evenings per week for biology during the second six months, since biology included botany and zoology. They didn't close over the summer period because some of their income came from giving school pupils additional tuition in the summer. Although my nursing hours were still awkward and quite long, I was the charge nurse and therefore in charge of the duty roster, so could always ensure that I was off on the relevant evenings.

I found A level physics difficult with only O level maths and I had to spend more time on the physics than on the chemistry. However, I passed both, and surprisingly did better in physics. The grades were adequate passes but not the high grades usually expected of applicants coming straight from school. Then I set about the A level biology but this time just using the textbook and my two nights a week for the laboratory work.

I had to apply to Glasgow University before I sat the examination but indicated that I'd be submitting my biology result when it became available. As before I required two references but didn't want anyone associated with the hospital to know I was applying to read medicine. In retrospect, that was silly and naive. I was working in a hospital that wasn't only a nurse training hospital but also a university teaching hospital, and I was working with influential consultants who were part of the university teaching staff. The principal of Glasgow Tutorial College and my biology tutor seemed like a good idea so I went to them for references and submitted my application.

At about this time a flat became available to rent in Hillhead Street, Glasgow adjacent to the university and we had friends, Jack and Pauline Connelly, who had a similar flat just around the corner. They had some influence with the letting agent and we were able to get the flat. We moved there, not with any real expectation of my getting a place in medical school, but ever hopeful. By this time I was determined that I wanted to be doctor and decided that if I was refused I would do what was needed to get better grades and try again next year.

The decision arrived in late August 1966. I had not been accepted and I hadn't been rejected, but was on the *waiting list*. The letter informed me that this didn't guarantee me a place but that more than 80 per cent of those on the list would be successful. My understanding is that all the available places are offered to two groups. First, those who already have the necessary grades are given a firm offer but they may have applied to more than one university, so may or may not take the place. The other group is made up of those who are given conditional acceptances depending on their exam results. Some of those may not get the required grades. The places vacated by those who opt to go to other universities or don't get the grades are offered to those on the waiting list.

Dilemma

The same day I got my letter Mr Phillips was admitted with a problem with his big toe joints and Mr MacDougall took him to theatre. In an unconventional procedure he straightened the joints under anaesthetic and put the foot in plaster. The following day the patient was complaining of severe pain in the foot and asked to have the plaster removed. We tried the foot in various positions, checked for pressure areas and gave him painkillers, all to no avail. I rang the Victoria but couldn't contact Mr MacDougall, so I spoke to his registrar who said he wouldn't take responsibility for giving me permission to remove the plaster. Mr Freeman, another consultant, was visiting the ward that day so I asked his advice, but he wouldn't get involved with another consultant's patient. I made several more unsuccessful attempts to speak to Mr MacDougall.

Meanwhile the patient was becoming increasingly distressed and Sister Thomson's words were ringing in my ears: 'You have a duty to relieve pain and if you have the means to do so, you must do it and take the consequences, no matter who refuses to give you permission.' I took the plaster cutters and removed the plaster, with immediate relief for the patient and immediate anxiety for me.

At the next ward round two days later I explained what I'd done and Mr MacDougall looked displeased but didn't say anything to me. However, he told Matron and she called me to her office for an explanation, which I gave to the best of my ability. She accepted it and that was the end of the matter, or so I thought.

Confidentiality

A few days later and feeling a little more confident of the possibility of getting into medical school, I was chatting to my part-time staff nurse, Ann McLean, over coffee. I mentioned the possibility that I could be leaving soon and she took this to mean for the tutors' course.

She said, 'I don't want to disappoint you. But you may not get the secondment you hope for. Miss Locke doesn't always keep her promises. She may have made that promise to get you to stay on but that doesn't mean she'll keep it.'

At last, after keeping my real hopes secret for so long, I felt confident enough to tell one person, so I said, 'I'm telling you this in strict confidence because I don't want it generally known until I know if I'll be accepted, but I'm on the waiting list to read medicine at Glasgow University. Although I've not been guaranteed a place, I have at least an eighty per cent chance of being successful.'

'You have my word,' she agreed.

The following week Mr MacDougall did his ward round as usual and after the normal discussions about the patients he said, 'I hear you've applied to Glasgow University to do medicine.' He asked me a bit about my educational qualifications and after a brief discussion he wished me all the best and left.

How did he know? It turned out Mrs McLean had told Miss Gunn, the deputy matron, in confidence. She told Miss Whyte, the matron, in confidence and she told Mr MacDougall, in confidence. I learned later that he went straight to the Victoria Infirmary to his secretary and dictated a letter to the University recommending me.

This was a surprise to me in view of the incident with Mr Phillips but I discovered later that Mr MacDougall had spoken to his registrar about the incident and Mr Freeman, the other consultant who had refused to get involved, had mentioned it to him. As a result, instead of holding it against me he was impressed by my making a firm clinical decision and taking decisive action on behalf of my patient.

Interview

A week after my conversation with Mr MacDougall, I received a letter from the university inviting me to come for an interview. That was encouraging but very daunting. I don't perform very well at interviews or oral examinations.

One of the early questions was, 'Why did you not do things in the usual way and study for Highers at school?' I suppose pupils going up from school are primed to some extent, so will have an idea of the kind of questions they'll face and the sort of answers expected from them, but I didn't know what to expect and wasn't very clear in some of my answers. I said something like, 'I'm not sure but my mother always said, "People like us can't be doctors". I remember her coming to me when I was eleven and saying, "You don't want to go to the Academy, do you, son?" and my saying, "No," and that was it settled. I was going to the local junior secondary school and there was no way of doing Highers from there.'

Another interviewer came to my rescue and said, 'Was it a cultural thing? Your parents were working class and didn't even consider sending you to a senior secondary school?'

'Yes, that's it.'

The next comment from yet another interviewer should not have been unexpected but it was. He said, 'It's taken you a long time to get your educational qualifications. You'll need to work a lot faster than that if you come up to University. Do you think you'll be able to cope with that?' I knew his comment was true, but I hadn't anticipated it and was a bit taken aback. I soon composed myself and pointed out that although it had taken me five years to get six O levels, this had started out simply as an exercise in improving my educational qualifications with no timescale in mind, and I'd done it while working full-time and undertaking my nursing studies. For my main argument I stated, 'I'm confident that I've passed the A level biology exam and that means I've taken physics, chemistry and biology from O level to A level in one year while working full-time, whereas it normally takes two years of full-time study. I am confident I will keep up with the University course.'

The final question was, 'What do you think of the state of medicine today?' This really threw me and I mumbled some comments about doctors' working conditions, suggesting that GPs and consultants appeared to have satisfactory conditions but junior doctors' hours were too long. I don't think this was something they expected to hear but with hindsight my answer would still be the same but said with more conviction. They thanked me for coming and said they would wait for the results of my last exam.

Image 8-6: University of Glasgow
from Kelvingrove Bowling Green

When my results came in I had passed comfortably and with a better grade than for physics and chemistry. Soon after that I received a letter telling me I had been accepted to study medicine at the University of Glasgow. I thanked those who had given me references and in particular Mr MacDougall. I will never know if I would have been accepted without his recommendation, but I'm sure it more or less guaranteed my acceptance.

Parents

So far I hadn't told my parents about my dream of becoming a doctor in case I couldn't get into medical school. My mother in particular was proud of the progress I had made in nursing, but becoming a doctor was a totally different matter and the last thing I wanted was to hear the words, 'We told you so'.

Once I knew I'd been accepted, Mary and I went to see them to let them know. My father rarely showed his approval unless it was something to do with preaching. He said something along the lines of, 'You'll be getting proud after this.'

My mother was pleased that I'd been accepted but expressed her concern. 'Do you think you'll manage all the hard studying? You'll be with a lot of very clever people.'

To me, getting into medical school was the biggest hurdle and I said, 'It won't be easy but I'm confident I can succeed.'

Chapter 9

University

More Exams?

I was now about to become a full-time student so handed in my notice at Philipshill and arranged to have a short holiday in Girvan with Mary and her parents. Then out of the blue I received a telephone call from a secretary at the university. She said, 'Congratulations on getting a place. Since you have A levels in physics, chemistry and biology you are eligible to sit the examination for direct entry to second year.' She told me the date of the examination and how much it would cost for me to sit it. This presented me with three problems. To stand any chance I would need intensive revision of chemistry and physics, and there was no time for that. The date coincided with our holiday, and if I paid for the exam I couldn't afford to go on holiday.

There was no time to discuss it with Mary or her parents, and I was so delighted at having been accepted I didn't really care about exemption from the first year. I told her, 'It's all right, I don't want to sit the exam, I'll do the first year.'

She seemed surprised and said, 'But your place is guaranteed either way. If you pass you'll go straight into second year but if you fail you'll go into the first.' I assured her I was more than happy to do the first year and that was that. Although I'd read the regulations I'd forgotten about this mechanism for A level students.

Making the Transition

By this time Mary was pregnant with our first child and she had dreadful pregnancy sickness, not just bad morning sickness but a condition called *hyperemesis gravidarum* throughout the pregnancy, so had to give up her work. (The Duchess of Cambridge famously suffered from this condition, but with no financial ill effects.) Mary unfortunately received no medical help for this since the memory of the thalidomide tragedy was still prominent in the minds of doctors, and they were reluctant to prescribe any drugs during pregnancy.

I had to set about applying for a grant. Being twenty-eight and married I was entitled to a married mature student's grant which was a bit more than the regular grant for younger students. Even with that we knew it was going to be difficult financially. I had been running an old car as a charge nurse but this was no longer an option so it had to be sold early in the first year.

We were given a timetable of lectures and a list of books and equipment we would need. Although there was an allowance for books in the grant, it didn't cover the cost of the recommended books. Equipment was simply a dissection kit for biology. Subjects in the first year were physics, chemistry, and biology, similar to A levels but with a much greater emphasis on organic chemistry, and biology involved a lot more dissection, and greater emphasis on zoology. There were about 200 students in each year of medicine, and for laboratory work we were divided into groups of four or five.

I soon found that on many university courses, especially in the arts, students had much more time for study during the day. They appeared to spend very short periods in lectures but then had lots of time to study. With medicine as with other science-based subjects a lot of time was spent in laboratories as well as in lecture theatres so there was no free time at all during the day. This meant that all of our studying had to be done in the evenings, and I had to devise a strategy for spending time with Mary as well as studying.

From early on we discovered that money was indeed tight and we had to find another means of supplementing our income. We had a spare room so we decided we would have a boarder to live with us. We advertised and quickly found a suitable student completing a business studies course. Mary continued to suffer from hyperemesis gravidarum throughout her pregnancy, with the result that I had to do much of the cooking, both for ourselves and our boarder, and I served his meals.

In the past I had found that writing notes helped me to learn so I decided that I would take rough notes during lectures and rewrite them at home in neat handwriting. This was fine in theory but I soon discovered that I was getting behind with my writing up, so had to take notes in the lectures that I could read at home without transcribing. Lectures at university were very different from the teaching in the School of Building and in the Schools of Nursing, where they spoke slowly and wrote what we needed to note on a blackboard. Here they spoke at normal speed and used blackboards or overhead projectors purely for illustrations. This is probably why doctors are such bad writers. Six years of writing very fast at the expense of neatness leads to bad writing habits!

Routine

I soon settled into a routine. Coming home from lectures or laboratories around 5 pm I set about preparing the evening meal for all of us. Once the meal was over I settled down to studying around 7 pm. I studied till about 9 pm and then spent time with Mary. Many students did very little studying in the early parts of the term and then crammed towards the end for the examinations. This method didn't suit me and I found that doing a little on a regular basis was much more effective, resulting in my passing all my examinations.

Rowdy Students

One aspect of being a university student I found puzzling and disconcerting was the behaviour of many of the students in the lecture theatres. Sometimes when a person who was more junior or didn't convey sufficient authority was giving the lecture, or when a fellow student had an announcement to make, there would be outbreaks of disorder with shouting and banging of desks. There were even occasions when the lecturer had to give up and leave, and fellow students trying to make announcements were reduced to tears. It must be stated that not all behaved in this way, indeed it was probably a minority but it was a substantial minority.

As a mature student ten years older than the average student, I tried to justify this by thinking of it as just youthful high spirits. But was it? I had attended lectures in the School of Building with fellow students between the ages of sixteen and twenty-one, all impeccably behaved. All worked hard on building sites during the other days of the week, and applied themselves during their day at college despite many not wanting to be there. They worked hard and often played hard but only in their own time. I had attended lectures and worked with student nurses of a similar age. There was no such rowdiness with them. Indeed they happily subjected themselves to almost military discipline in lectures, and especially in the wards.

Obstetric Emergency

As Mary approached term our friend Jack Connelly, who lived just round the corner, gave us a spare set of his car keys and told us to use his car if she went into labour at night. Sure enough, during the second term of my first year, in March 1967, Mary went into labour in the middle of the night and I drove her to the Queen Mother's Maternity Hospital.

This was a time when midwives and maternity units were being encouraged to allow expectant fathers to be present at the birth. They paid lip service to it, but in practice it wasn't encouraged. As soon as Mary was admitted to the antenatal ward and settled, I was advised to go home and telephone in the morning. I telephoned at 8 am to be told she was making slow but steady progress but was not nearly fully dilated. Following my first lecture at 10 am I rang again to be told she was not making much progress and they were giving her an epidural injection to relieve the pain before trying to assist with the delivery. There was unlikely to be any news for a couple of hours so I went to my next lecture but continued to telephone every hour or so. I was getting increasingly anxious with each delay but was given reassurances that they had things under control and it would soon all be over.

Things did not go well with Mary. The epidural didn't work so she was put on Entonox (gas and air) but no one had noticed that the gas cylinder was empty so she was getting no pain relief at all. The baby was in the wrong position which made a natural delivery almost impossible. In the first instance a special suction apparatus known as ventouse was used. This managed to pull a piece of scalp from the baby but did nothing to help the delivery. The next thing they tried was the use of forceps known as Keilland's forceps, but because Mary was not fully dilated this resulted in severe damage to her cervix and very serious loss of blood.

Mary was conscious throughout all this and because epidural anaesthesia had failed and the Entonox was non-existent she became very distressed and almost lost consciousness. Then there were signs of foetal distress and she was taken for an emergency Caesarean section. Eventually at 12.45 pm on 7 March we were blessed with a lovely baby daughter whom we named Eunice Elizabeth.

It would have been a great comfort for Mary to have me present and I would have loved to have been there. However in the circumstances I would have been sent out of the delivery room as soon as problems arose.

Parenthood

Mary didn't see her baby for long because within minutes of the birth Eunice was taken to neonatal intensive care and Mary to adult intensive care. I was allowed to visit Mary and was taken for a brief visit to look through the glass window at my baby daughter, but not to touch her. Conscious of my father's lack of interaction with us, I resolved to spend as much time as I could with my child or children throughout their childhood. After two days Mary was taken in a wheelchair to see her precious baby.

Mary's parents came to stay with me while Mary was in hospital and they were very helpful but Mary's mother, who had a heart of gold, was used to organising her own home and brought that organisation to my home. Her father always said, 'My name's on the *outside* of the door at our home,' meaning his name was on the nameplate but that was where his authority ended. His wife ruled once inside the door.

With the best of intentions she took over and I found that very distressing since, to some extent, I was a creature of habit and didn't like my routines being disrupted, or my role in the home being usurped. At least that's what it felt like! The final indignity came when I came home from lectures one day to find I had been moved out of our bedroom into a spare room. She had done this in consideration, so that I could have peaceful nights and not be disturbed by the new baby in the house.

There was no way I was going to be separated from my wife or my baby, but I couldn't bring myself to tell her. When I went to visit Mary that evening she noticed I was upset, and I explained to her why. She soon put this right with her mum and I was moved back into my own bedroom again.

Mary was in hospital for about two weeks after the birth of Eunice. When she came home from hospital she was still very weak and required a lot of help. However we gradually settled into a routine with both of us sharing looking after Eunice and doing the cooking.

I successfully completed the first year without failing any of the exams and managed to get a distinction in chemistry. Getting exemption from the first year, and therefore having one year less to study would have been very useful. However, I think having that year going over familiar material, almost like a revision but with some additional new work, was very helpful in letting me settle into university life and fatherhood.

Back to Nursing

Having a wife and now a new baby to support I clearly had to work during the summer break and applied to go back to Philipshill Hospital to do holiday relief work. They were happy to have me and I spent some of the time doing relief in the two male wards and the children's ward. I also spent some time in theatre. Theatre Sister had resigned and her replacement hadn't yet been appointed but there was an efficient staff nurse in charge. She didn't want the post because she was soon to be married and would be leaving. As a charge nurse I was senior to her but her theatre experience was superior to mine. We agreed that she would continue in charge and I would assist.

When Mr MacDougall saw me he looked puzzled and said to me, 'Was it difficult?'

I don't think I was very clear when I replied, 'It wasn't easy but I've completed the first year.' He didn't say anything else but did look a little disappointed and probably thought I had failed and left. I learned later from one of the sisters that he wrote to the university to find out about my progress. After he'd received a reply he went back quite excitedly and told her that I was doing extremely well.

At this time there were reports of prowlers around the nurses' quarters at night. Matron called me to her office and asked if I would be willing to do a spell on night duty so they had a man around. I was willing to do this. Being the night duty sister/charge nurse involved being responsible for the whole hospital and doing ward rounds, supervising the night duty staff nurses and also supervising the Nurses' and Sisters' Homes. This latter part of the duties I found a little awkward, being male. I had to go to the nurses' and sisters' quarters and check that they were all in by the required time (10 pm) and then make sure the outside doors were securely locked. Resident nurses were allowed a late pass each week and could be out till midnight but had to report to me so that I could let them in. One of my duties in the morning was to go around the student nurses' quarters knocking on the doors to make sure they were up in time.

I didn't find any evidence of prowlers while I was on night duty but the rumours, if they were rumours, disappeared. One piece of night-time activity I did find myself getting involved in, however, related not to a two-legged prowler but a four-legged one. There was a gatehouse at the entrance to the hospital and this was occupied by a Health Board official. He bought a horse for his daughter and the poor animal was overfed and under-exercised. It managed to free itself very late one night and went galloping up and down the grounds of the hospital churning up the grass at an alarming rate.

The owner came to me for help but I know nothing about capturing runaway horses. However, two of the night nurses were competent horsewomen and they came with me. After a lot of running around in the dark we eventually managed to catch it and get it back in the stable. And that's the only horseplay I experienced while supervising the nurses' quarters!

Just before leaving to go back to university I learned that the post of Theatre Sister had been filled, except that it wasn't a sister but a charge nurse. I was delighted to hear that one of my former fellow student nurses from Hairmyres, Bob Murray, had been appointed.

Second Year

Doing that spell of night duty at Philipshill gave me the idea that I could do one night per week during term time, and more during the Christmas and Easter breaks. I would need a car again but with the new income from the student boarder and my extra work, that would be possible. I asked Matron and she was happy to have me, but the only night available was a Sunday night.

Being a charge nurse and therefore responsible for the whole hospital I wasn't overseeing a ward but did my work in the office. After taking a report from Matron or her assistant when I reported for duty, I read up on any matters that needed close supervision; who had operations that day and if any patients were particularly ill. The ward lights were usually put out around 10 pm and I did my rounds sometime shortly after that. With five wards to visit this usually took about an hour, and then it was staff mealtime.

If all was quiet and there were no major problems in the wards I was usually able to go back to the office and do some of my paperwork. I must confess that this was a very difficult time and I often had a snooze for an hour or so. There was another quick round of the wards in the small hours but this usually involved simply going up to the entrance to the ward and having a quick word with the staff nurse on duty. There was a full ward round in the morning and then a report had to be written up before Matron or her deputy came on duty.

There was also the question of making sure the student nurses were up on time. I often asked one of the auxiliary nurses to do this for me and I did some of her duties. Since I was working Sunday nights, when I came off duty on Monday morning I drove straight to university to my lectures. I had a flask of tea and a sandwich which I consumed in the car on the way. This was fine in the morning but afternoon lectures were very difficult indeed and I found myself frequently nodding off and my pen skidding across the paper while I tried to take notes.

This arrangement continued through my second and third years and ended when I moved to Glasgow Eye Infirmary in 1969.

The second year subjects were anatomy, physiology and biochemistry. The pattern of second year lectures was pretty much the same as the first with a mixture of lectures and laboratory work.

The practical anatomy was interesting. There were 200 medical students in our year and we went into a very large room which had fifty tables laid out with a dead body on each. As a nurse I had dealt with death frequently and, as mentioned, associated the smell of Dettol with death. In this case the smell was not of Dettol but formaldehyde with which the bodies were preserved. We were divided into groups of four to each body and dissecting a body was to be our practical anatomy project for the whole of the second year. These practical sessions were supervised by postgraduate doctors who were hoping to become surgeons and were spending time working in the anatomy department to fine-tune their own knowledge of anatomy.

Intercalated Science Degree

Those students who reached a high standard in their first and second years were offered the opportunity of taking time out of the medical course to study for a BSc in a medical science such as anatomy, physiology, immunology or biochemistry. This was usually an additional one year. I was offered the opportunity and I thought long and hard about it. There was a certain prestige in doing this and it would no doubt enhance the career prospects of those who undertook the additional studies. The grant could be extended for an extra year to cover this and Mary and I discussed the pros and cons.

When I thought about being a doctor as a child it was a family doctor I had in mind, but with my interest in orthopaedics and being a father creating an interest in working with children we had an open mind as to the future direction of my career at this stage. Reluctantly I had to agree with Mary when she said that the extra degree was less important than getting medically qualified as soon as possible, and I declined the offer.

Clinical Studies

First and second years had comprised preclinical studies but the third year marked the start of clinical studies. We continued some of the preclinical work, especially biochemistry and pathology. The clinical work involved attending lectures, as with all subjects, but instead of laboratory work we were taught by clinicians in the wards seeing real patients.

We were divided into groups of approximately ten and attached to a particular consultant and his team. This meant that we were scattered across the four main teaching hospitals in Glasgow. There was a certain amount of choice and I was able to spend most, but not all, of my clinical time in the Western Infirmary, which meant I could walk there from home. Teaching usually took the form of the consultant running a tutorial in a side room. Then we were taken into the ward as a group and shown a patient or patients with the condition being taught. Taking case histories was part of the learning process and this involved sitting down with the patient to take their history from the beginning.

My nursing experience was obviously helpful here but the approach was completely different. Apart from the fact that we were learning things in so much more detail, we had to learn to approach it almost like detective work. In nursing when we learned about medical conditions we were told the condition and learned its signs and symptoms. Similarly when we saw patients, someone else had already made the diagnosis. In medicine we were learning how to arrive at a diagnosis for ourselves. In other words we would be given a symptom or a set of symptoms and had to learn what conditions might possibly produce those symptoms. This is known as *differential diagnosis*.

The Beadle's Lost

A beadle is an officer in the church who carries out certain practical and ceremonial duties. *Materia medica* is the study of drugs. This was one of our subjects and these lectures were given in the large lecture theatre to the full class of 200.

I was friendly with Tom, a rather earnest young man who appeared to lack any kind of filter between his brain and his mouth. What he thought was what he said and I was sitting beside him near the back of the theatre.

We were being lectured on methyldopa, a drug widely used in the treatment of high blood pressure at that time. The lecturer was going over the side effects and he gave us some examples from clinical practice. In one example he referred to a church minister who, after being given methyldopa, came back with some unpleasant side effects.

The lecturer quoted the minister and along with the other side effects, Tom appeared to hear him say, 'I've lost my beadle'.

He immediately stood up and called out, 'Excuse me, how can it make him lose his beadle?'

The whole lecture theatre erupted in laughter, and the lecturer replied, 'The patient had loss of libido.'

'Oh!' said Tom, 'what's libido?'

There was more laughter and I said, 'Sit down, Tom and I'll explain after the lecture.'

Breast Examination

Tom and I were in the same small group for our first surgery teaching. The surgeon, Mr Brown, taught us how to examine a breast. He then took us to a brave lady who had volunteered to be the guinea pig and demonstrated the procedure. Then he said to Tom, 'Now let me see you examine Mrs Alexander in the same way.'

Tom went forward and putting earlier instruction into practice he attempted to engage his patient in conversation. 'Good morning, Mrs Alexander, thank you for allowing me to examine you,' he said, 'you have lovely breasts.' She looked embarrassed as we cringed. Then gently, slowly and lightly he ran his fingers over the breast. Starting at the axilla he moved over the top, then under the breast and towards the nipple.

The patient looked alarmed and Mr Brown said, 'Stop.' He apologised to the patient and then took us aside. He rebuked Tom for not paying attention to his teaching, and added, 'That was meant to be a medical encounter, not social!'

Change of Hospital

By the end of my third year the finances were getting difficult even with the extra income and we had to sell the car again. This would make travelling to Philipshill Hospital difficult and not very practical. So I applied to Glasgow Eye Infirmary for full-time temporary summer work, as it was within walking distance. I was accepted to start in July 1969. Since our boarder was a student he went home during the summer and we didn't have that extra income during the vacation.

Further Thoughts on Sexism

We decided to decorate the flat during the summer break while the boarder was away. One evening I was on a stepladder hanging wallpaper in the hall when the doorbell rang. Mary answered and a smartly dressed young woman of a similar age to us stood at the door. She asked if this was where Jimmy and Mary Graham lived and introduced herself as Grace Sanders, a colleague of Nancy McWee. Mary invited her in and I greeted her from the ladder still holding on to the wallpaper. After I had hung that length of paper I cleaned myself up a bit and joined them in the lounge. Nancy McWee, a friend from Mary's church in Cambuslang, was a sister tutor in Glasgow Royal Infirmary, one of the major teaching hospitals in Glasgow.

Grace too was a sister tutor at the Royal but she wanted to be a doctor. She said, 'The way nursing training is going nowadays I'm training my students to be *baby doctors*.' Asked if she meant midwives or paediatric nurses she replied, 'No, I mean they're being taught highly academic material and aren't getting enough hands-on nursing experience. They're gradually taking over procedures doctors normally do and becoming specialised in small areas of medicine. I'm not happy doing this and would rather be a doctor myself.'

'You're highly qualified with your nursing and teaching qualifications. Do you have the necessary Highers for entry to medicine?' I enquired.

'Yes, and I applied to Glasgow University but was rejected despite having good references from two consultants.'

'Did you get an interview?' I asked.

'Yes. They were very frosty and told me I had already received considerable help from the state with my training in nursing and midwifery followed by two years at Edinburgh University for the tutors' course. "You're providing an excellent service teaching future generations of nurses. Continue to do that," was the parting shot.' I was surprised but asked what advice she thought I could give. She replied, 'How did you manage to get accepted?'

I gave her a brief account of my journey and suggested, 'Look at your Highers again to see if you can add another and improve your grades. Then apply to a wide range of medical schools and perhaps one will accept you.'

This encounter with Grace made me reflect on my acceptance. Without being unkind to Archie MacDougall, was there an element of sexism in his unsolicited recommendation of me? Would he have made the same approach on behalf of one of the sisters in similar circumstances? Would the selection committee have accepted me if I were female?

Fourth Year

At the end of the summer break in 1969 I went into fourth-year studies and needed to continue to work, so I applied for a part-time night duty post at the Eye Infirmary and was given a Friday night. This was ideal because I could come home from lectures for a few hours before going out to work. As I had found at Philipshill, the wee small hours were very difficult and the desire to sleep overwhelming. This time I was on a ward and someone had to be alert at all times. However, when the patients were all settled and the staff meals were over it was often possible to have a short sleep on the chair in the middle of the ward, taking it in turns with the auxiliary nurse, one having a snooze and the other staying alert. Since I was coming off duty on a Saturday morning I was able to go to bed and sleep for a few hours.

In the Christmas and Easter breaks and in the summer break between third and fourth year I was able to increase my hours to full-time.

Another Baby

Fourth year was entirely clinical and we continued to learn our subjects in greater depth and covering an increasingly wide range of specialties. Mary was already pregnant with our second child when I started, and the sickness was just as bad as the first time. Like then, it continued throughout the entire pregnancy. This time she had the complication of looking after a two-year-old toddler as well. It wasn't uncommon for me to come in from lectures to find her with Eunice in her arms and her head in the sink vomiting. The sight and especially the smell of food made her worse but she soldiered on and did her best, starting to prepare the evening meal till I came in and took over. We still had our student so it was essential that we maintained a routine.

Mary's obstetrician was concerned that there may be problems with the delivery because of the damage done to her cervix by the Kielland's forceps when Eunice was delivered, but it was difficult to be certain until nearer term. The decision was made to take her to theatre a few weeks before her due date for an examination under anaesthetic. This was on 8 November 1969 and as she was coming round from the anaesthetic she could hear a voice in the mist saying, 'Wake up, Mrs Graham, you have a lovely baby boy.' They had discovered there was too much damage to allow her to go into labour, so carried out a Caesarean section there and then. We were, of course, delighted and called him Norman James. He too went to neonatal intensive care because he had been born before term but we were both able to see him and hold him regularly. I was so overjoyed at having a son and a daughter, and I just knew that, unlike my father, I would want to spend as much time as possible with them.

Mary's parents came over again to help look after Eunice while Mary and Norman were still in hospital and that was a great help. This time her mother knew not to try to turn me out of our bedroom. Mary needed a lot of help at first because her wound was painful but we soon settled into a routine again.

Something Completely Different

The summer vacation between my fourth and fifth years was the last we would have, because studies continued from fifth year into sixth without a break. Since by that time I'd been working and studying in health care for about fourteen years I thought it would be a useful experience to spend this last summer break in a different type of occupation. Mary's brother, Roddy, was a foreman in a local tobacco factory and they took on students during the summer. He was able to get me started doing temporary summer work.

I did have some reservations about working in this environment since there was a growing awareness of the link between smoking and certain illnesses, especially lung cancer. However the link was not so strong at that time and the tobacco industry was still producing its own counter arguments. What's more, many, if not most doctors and nurses were still smoking with no real efforts to stop. To illustrate this, towards the end of our fourth year, we had tutorials on the subject of cancer including possible causes, signs, symptoms, investigations and available treatments. At the end of one tutorial, the senior registrar who was leading it came over to chat with two of the students he knew personally.

His greeting was, 'I'm gasping for a cigarette. Can you lend me one?' They both reached for their jacket pockets and produced a packet of cigarettes each. This senior registrar was recognised as someone who was going places and had a bright future.

Perhaps I was making excuses for myself but I thought, making cigarettes can't be all that bad if he smokes. Although we couldn't foretell the future he was appointed as consultant in oncology soon after that and quickly became Professor. He rose to a senior position in the Department of Health in Scotland and later in England and Wales, receiving a knighthood for his work.

I was assigned to the cigar factory and my task was to chop up tobacco leaf for the cigars. This involved getting a bogey full of the leaf and putting the leaf into one end of a machine, watching it get chopped up and come out the other end into another bogey which I took to another section. I did this all day, every day, and it was mind-numbingly boring. The men working in the factory went off for frequent toilet breaks, which usually meant going off for a smoke, and I fully understood the need for them to break the monotony. Working as an unskilled labourer in the factory I was paid about the same as I had been paid as a charge nurse in the NHS.

By the time I came to the end of my ten weeks or so of working in the factory I was looking forward to getting back to my medical studies. It made me really appreciate the type of work I had done in the past, and was hoping to do again in the future.

Fifth year began in October 1970. Ironically, towards the end of my fifth year there was a competitive examination for the top student in each of the small groups for a prestigious prize. I was put forward as the top student in Dr Olav Kerr's group. We were asked to examine patients and identify equipment or other relevant items and then discuss them with the examiner. One exhibit was a cigarette and the question was, 'What is this? Discuss six conditions associated with it.' I was suitably chastened and I didn't get the prize, but just being in the group chosen to compete was honour enough, possibly a bit like an actor being nominated for an Oscar but not actually winning it.

We still had our student boarder and I went back to doing my one night per week at Glasgow Eye Infirmary. We obviously had additional expenses with another baby in the family, but since we were given a small addition to the grant and were now eligible for Family Allowance (the predecessor of Child Benefit), our financial situation remained much the same. At that time Family Allowance wasn't awarded for the first child.

Obstetric Moans

We are aware of moans in labour wards; not moans of complaint but moans of pain. As a mere male I could never experience the pain of labour but I have had gallstones with biliary colic and I did a fair bit of moaning. We have a saying in medicine: 'The pain of renal colic or biliary colic is the nearest a man will get to labour pains.'

We did obstetrics in the fifth year and as with most subjects we had a choice of hospital for small group practical work. I, with another seven, chose Stobhill Hospital on the north side of Glasgow. My reasons were partly because I could arrange a lift from a fellow student who had a car and partly because a lot of babies were delivered there. We had practical work books which had to be signed to prove we had participated in a prescribed number of deliveries. But medical students were competing with student midwives and Stobhill had more deliveries and fewer student midwives than some of the other hospitals.

We gelled well as a group and were enjoying our obstetric experience, when halfway through the term we were informed that we were being moved to the world famous Glasgow Royal Maternity Hospital, affectionately known as Rottenrow, after the street it was on. By this time we had gained most of the required delivery experience but still needed more.

No explanation for the move was given but I suspect it was to give the Rottenrow group access to the greater number of deliveries at Stobhill. We were not happy bunnies because we'd been moved without explanation and because it proved difficult to get the few deliveries we still needed in our new environment. There was a suspicion that the staff midwives and sisters were favouring their own student midwives.

We were a group of eight composed of four Scots, two English, one Northern Irish and one Central American. With the teaching sessions over for the day, we were sitting around discussing the teaching, and deciding which two would stay behind for the evening to try to get one of the elusive deliveries. We were feeling very disgruntled and were *enjoying* a right good moan at the perceived injustice. 'The University authorities have been so unfair disturbing our carefully laid plans. The midwives are being so unfair for not giving us a fair share of the deliveries.'

While we were in the midst of our little moan Abdul, the Central American chap, said, 'Right, there's no point sitting around complaining. We need to do something about it.'

Sally, the Northern Irish girl joined with him and responded, 'I agree, we need to divide into two groups. Abdul can lead one group and go to the Professor of Obstetrics and complain about them moving us, and I can lead the second group and go to Matron to register a complaint about our unfair treatment by the midwives.' The remaining six of us just sat in silent disbelief thinking, are they seriously suggesting we should complain?

Pauline, one of the English girls said, 'Perhaps we should take some time to think about it,' but Abdul insisted that we needed to act quickly to try to get back to Stobhill.

Then I spoke up. 'We're not in the business of starting revolutions. We've had a right good moan, but now that we've got it off our chests we need to accept the situation. If those who were here need access to the deliveries in Stobhill then seeing as we've achieved most of ours, that's only fair. We've no proof the midwives are showing favouritism to their own students. I suggest we accept the situation and settle down to making the most of our studies here.' There was a look of relief on the faces of the other five and we outvoted our two revolutionaries. They weren't too happy because they just couldn't understand why we complained but weren't prepared to act. The fact was, having a right good moan was therapeutic and enabled us to settle down in our new surroundings.

Déjà Vu

Two days later, on our next visit to the hospital, the place was buzzing with talk of a poor mother, Jean Livingstone, who was in intensive care following a very difficult delivery in which she almost died and almost lost the baby.

Jean had been admitted in labour the previous day but the labour failed to proceed as it should due to the baby being in the wrong position. He was occipito-posterior, meaning he was facing forwards instead of backwards. Attempts at helping the delivery using suction apparatus known as ventouse failed just as it had with Mary. Keilland's forceps were used to try to turn and pull the baby out at the same time. This failed, and in the process Jean's cervix was badly lacerated causing severe blood loss just as it had with Mary. There were signs of foetal distress and she was taken for emergency Caesarean section and given a blood transfusion.

Both mother and baby survived but only just, and only after an extensive period in intensive care for both, just as in the case of Mary and Eunice. We were taught on the subject subsequently and in particular about the dangers of using forceps, especially Keilland's forceps, without being absolutely certain the cervix is fully dilated. Being in the same hospital where this incident occurred certainly helped impress the subject on the minds of my fellow students. It was already impressed on mine due to the experience of Mary and Eunice but to some extent it vindicated our move to Rottenrow.

Disasters

The following year was an unhappy, eventful year in Glasgow with three significant events: there was the

Ibrox disaster, the fire which destroyed the wards of Glasgow Eye Infirmary, and the Clarkston disaster.

The Ibrox disaster occurred at the end of the annual New Year old firm derby between Glasgow Rangers and Glasgow Celtic on 2 January 1971 when a crash barrier on Stairway 13 of Ibrox Stadium collapsed, killing sixty-six people and injuring 200.

Later that January I received a telephone call to say I had to go to Canniesburn Hospital instead of the Eye

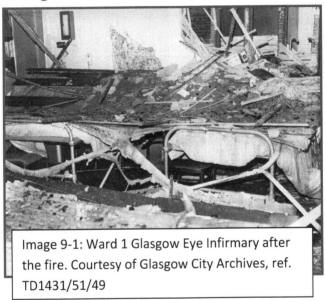

Image 9-1: Ward 1 Glasgow Eye Infirmary after the fire. Courtesy of Glasgow City Archives, ref. TD1431/51/49

Infirmary because there'd been a major fire and the wards had been totally destroyed. There was no loss of life, but the patients had to be evacuated and accommodation found for them at other Glasgow hospitals. A ward was made available for some in Canniesburn Hospital in Bearsden on the outskirts of Glasgow, and that was to be my base for the next few weeks. This wasn't so convenient since it involved a bus journey but was manageable.

Later that year an old Victorian hospital, Oakbank, became vacant and all the wards of the Eye Infirmary were reunited again on a temporary basis. My abiding memory of night duty there was of the cockroaches. They were among the largest I've seen anywhere and appeared in high numbers every night, usually around the kitchen, sluice and duty room, and I can still hear the crunching sound as we stood on them in a vain effort to be rid of them. Fortunately we didn't get too many in the wards among the patients. I continued my one-night-a-week night duty in Oakbank until after my finals in May and June 1972.

The Clarkston disaster came later in 1971 and was to briefly impact my own life—but more on this later.

Resident Student

During what would have been the summer break between fifth and sixth years we continued to attend lectures but were also expected to do more hands-on clinical work. There were some who went abroad to do that, especially to the USA, but most of us were able to undertake clinical work in the UK by doing locum cover for junior house officers in our own hospitals. My first post was at the Royal Alexandra Infirmary in Paisley covering for a junior house officer in surgery because I wanted to get as much experience as possible of adult surgery.

Most of the work was fairly routine and we had a senior house officer (SHO) or registrar available for advice, but as always in medicine we have to be ready for the unforeseen. I was called by the nurse one evening just after midnight to see a patient who'd been admitted earlier in the day with pain in his abdomen and back. He appeared to be stable but they decided to keep him in for observation. The nurse said his blood pressure had dropped and he was pale and clammy. I examined him and he was going into shock, so I set up an intravenous drip and called the SHO who thought he needed emergency surgery and called the registrar. Despite the intravenous drip with emergency plasma while blood was cross-matched ready for transfusion, the patient's blood pressure continued to fall rapidly and he died before theatre could be set up.

I was upset and asked myself, was this death my fault? Was there something else I could have done? Would he have died if there'd been a proper doctor on duty? The next two days were anxious for me as I waited for the result of the post-mortem examination. When available it revealed that he had a ruptured aortic aneurysm with catastrophic bleeding into the abdomen. This reassured me that there was nothing more I could have done, but I did wonder if perhaps earlier investigation in the form of X-rays and scans by those who admitted him may have resulted in life-saving surgery before the catastrophic bleed.

After a spell in Paisley I went to the Victoria Infirmary in Glasgow for another few weeks. These were residential posts doing the same hours as the junior doctors we were covering, so I wasn't able to continue doing my one night per week nursing. There was a supplement to the grant for the extra term, and we were paid a little money for the locum work, so that probably compensated for the loss of my income from nursing. Our student was away during the summer break as always.

One of the junior house officers I was covering at the Victoria Infirmary made his own home-brew beer, a large stock of which he kept on top of the wardrobe in his room. He invited me to take as much as I wanted. However not being much of a drinker, an odd glass of cider or very rarely a small glass of wine being my limit, I decided against taking up his offer.

Sixth year started in October 1971 and we had clinical teaching in surgery at the Victoria Infirmary. On 21 October as I was leaving with another student to get a bus home we became aware of ambulance sirens sounding, and many people being wheeled in on trolleys, far more than usual. A surgical registrar whom I had worked with while doing one of my surgical locums in the summer saw us and said, 'Wait, we need your help. There's been a major explosion and a high number of casualties are coming in.'

A build-up of gas in the basement of the shops at Clarkston Toll Shopping Centre had ignited causing an explosion, killing twenty-two people and seriously injuring around a hundred. Some went to A&E, some went to the wards and some to intensive care. We were given the task of putting up drips and giving intravenous fluids to those admitted.

At one point there was a short respite while we waited for the next lot to arrive and I remembered that Mary was expecting me home to make the dinner. It was

Image 9-2: Clarkston shops after the blast.

macaroni cheese that evening, and that was my speciality. I quickly telephoned her to let her know I was going to be late. My recipe was one I had learned from my mother and had never been written down, so I had to try to give her instructions guessing the quantities. I didn't make a very good job of passing them on to her so it turned out rather rubbery, and our boarder had to make do with fish and chips from the chippy when I eventually returned home that evening.

Very soon the next fleet of ambulances arrived and it was back to the serious business in hand. The Victoria Infirmary like all large hospitals had a major incident plan and this had been put into effect with great efficiency. Physicians, surgeons and anaesthetists rapidly

Image 9-3: Clarkston shops restored.

appeared as if from nowhere and casualties were handled appropriately and quickly. Perhaps they were fortunate in that the accident occurred at just the right time when almost all the senior staff were in the hospital and preparing to go home. Ironically the only person missing was Mr MacDougall, the senior orthopaedic surgeon, who was in overall charge of the major incident plan.

Finals and Graduation

The final examination was written and clinical with volunteer patients being present for us to take their histories and then examine them. The subjects for the final examinations were medicine, surgery, and obstetrics, other subjects having been completed in earlier years. We were told when the results would be available and that they would be posted on the noticeboard. When the day arrived almost all 200 of us gathered around scrambling to get a sight of the dreaded results.

There were screams of delight as, one by one, students realised they had passed, while for a few there were tears of disappointment because they had failed one or more subject. This was not the end of the line of course. They could resit in the autumn and if they failed that they could repeat the year so long as they had the financial resources to do so. I had passed all of my subjects which meant that I'd completed the course without failing a single subject and had achieved certificates of merit in most of them. So much for, 'People like us can't.' We can!

After passing the final examinations there was the graduation but before we could graduate we were required to assemble in the morning to take a form of the Hippocratic Oath.

I say, a form, because the original was in ancient Greek and called on the Greek gods and goddesses as witness. An English translation begins:

I swear by Apollo Physician and Asclepius and Hygieia and Panaceia and all the gods and goddesses, making them my witnesses, that I will fulfil according to my ability and judgement this oath and this covenant: . . .

I have the classical and modern versions of the Hippocratic Oath on my website: www.ascottishdoctor.com/university.

There are several modern versions but all follow similar underlying principles:

I solemnly promise:
That I will honour the Profession of Medicine;
That just as I have learned from those who preceded me, so will I instruct those who follow me in the science and the art of medicine;
That I will recognise my limitations and seek the counsel of others when they are more expert so as to fulfil my obligation to those who are entrusted to my care;
That I will not withdraw from my patients in their time of need;
That I will lead my life and practise my art with integrity and honour, using my power wisely;

*That whatsoever I shall see or hear of
the lives of my patients that is not fitting to be spoken, I will keep in confidence;*
*That into whatever house I shall enter,
it shall be for the good of the sick;*
*That I will maintain this sacred trust,
holding myself far aloof from wrong,
from corrupting, from the tempting of
others to vice;*
*That above all else I will serve the
highest interests of my patients
through the practice of my science and
my art;*
*That I will be an advocate for patients
in need and strive for justice in the
care of the sick.*
*I now turn to my calling, promising to
preserve its finest traditions, with the
reward of a long experience in the joy
of healing.*
*I make this promise freely and upon
my honour.*

Then we gathered in the magnificent Bute Hall with
two guests per student to have the degrees of Bachelor of
Medicine, Bachelor of Surgery conferred on us. These are
the basic qualifications of all UK medical graduates
allowing them to use the letters M.B., Ch.B. or B.M.,
B.Ch. with or without the full stops from the Latin

Medicinae Baccalaureus, Baccalaureus Chirurgiae if a graduate of many UK Universities including Glasgow.

Image 9-4: Bute Hall, University of Glasgow. Courtesy of University of Glasgow Photographic Unit, GB0248 PHU4/18

It's perhaps worth mentioning that in the UK medical doctors do not have a doctorate unlike in USA where the qualification is MD, Doctor of Medicine. There is an MD degree in the UK but it's a postgraduate degree conferred after guided research and presentation of a thesis. The title *Doctor* here is a courtesy title for the vast majority of medical doctors.

There was an official graduation dinner held in a Glasgow hotel. This was a lavish affair with after-dinner speeches, and many of the consultants on the university teaching staff attended. Mr MacDougall was there and made a point of speaking to me and congratulating me on my success, obviously very pleased that his protégé had been successful. I thanked him again for his interest in me and for that final push towards getting me into university. We chatted a bit about my plans for the future and he offered me sound advice, suggesting that as a mature person with two children I should go into general practice in one of the new health centres which were being developed. He said that GPs in that setting were developing special interests and I could have a special interest in orthopaedics.

Later we hosted our own private party with family and friends, held at our flat in Glasgow. Both sets of parents were delighted that I had graduated. My parents were pleased that I'd gone to university but had entertained reservations about my ability to successfully complete the course. However, my mother was immensely proud that I had become a doctor. I'm sure my father was too but it was not in his nature to show it. That might fill me with pride.

The next task was to get provisional registration with the General Medical Council in preparation for starting work as a junior hospital doctor. Successfully completing the six years of medical studies and obtaining the M.B., Ch.B. degrees enabled me to get that provisional registration. This in turn allowed me to work as a qualified doctor, but only in hospital under the supervision of a consultant. Full registration with the General Medical Council with the authority to practise without supervision was dependent on successful completion of two six-month posts in two of three disciplines. These were medicine and either surgery or obstetrics and gynaecology.

Junior Hospital Doctor

It was common practice to arrange junior house officer jobs during the final two years of study and competition for posts within the teaching hospitals was fierce. A future career in a hospital specialty was dependent on getting one of these prestigious posts. Often this was done by the consultant in charge of a unit inviting a student to be his or her house officer. There were, of course, many students with family members in the profession or who were personal friends of the consultants, so some obtained their positions this way. In other cases consultants chose students they liked or who had done well in their clinical studies within the small groups.

I had done a lot of my clinical medical studies in the Western Infirmary, Glasgow with Dr Olaf Kerr, consultant in charge of the unit, and he invited me to be one of his two house officers for the second six months of the preregistration year. This would be from February to

July 1973. Having two small children by this time, I was interested in children so applied for the post of junior house officer in surgery at the Royal Hospital for Sick Children, Yorkhill, Glasgow. They didn't offer posts to students but invited applications for junior house officer posts. I was successful and this post was to run from August 1972 through to the end of January 1973.

After completing the formalities and receiving the paperwork to say I was provisionally registered with the General Medical Council, I could call myself *doctor*. I resigned from my nursing post one week before the end of July to have a short family holiday before starting my first post on 1 August 1972. My lifelong ambition had been fulfilled and I could look forward to a career as a doctor.

How would I cope? I was used to taking responsibility as a charge nurse but then it was doctors who made the diagnosis, ordered investigations and prescribed treatment. Now as a doctor I'd be the one making life or death decisions. Now it was down to me.

To be continued.

Website

My website: www.ascottishdoctor.com contains additional information and more images, many of them in colour.

Contact

The author can be contacted via the website or at:
ascottishdoctor@gmail.com

Made in the USA
Middletown, DE
15 December 2015